Janet Giesselman
President and General Manager, Dow Oil and Gas
Jean Palmer Heck's methodology for effectively managing tough talks is unparalleled. These situations are always charged. You need a process for dealing with them and her CHECK system is the answer. Even after all my experience with tough talks, I learned from this book. Executives at my level will benefit from reading this.

Bob Daly
Senior Vice President, Toyota
Years in the turbulent auto industry have shown me the importance of being able to discuss both good and bad news while motivating associates along a path for success. These current economic times have made the need more urgent. This helpful book has case studies and ideas for tough talks that apply to all industries. If you manage people, read it.

Shep Hyken
Author of The Cult of the Customer, *a* Wall Street Journal *and* USA Today *best seller*
Simply put, if you are in any kind of management you need this book. While delivering tough news is never easy, you have to do it—even when you don't want to. Jean Palmer Heck's book, *Tough Talks in Tough Times*, provides you a specific process that shows you how to how to do so with style, respect, integrity, and confidence.

William C. Heyman
President and CEO, Heyman Associates, Inc.
In the spirit of Malcolm Gladwell's *Blink*, Jean Palmer Heck "thin slices" straight talk to employees during difficult times better than anyone I know. The sensitivities that *Tough Talks in Tough Times* uncovers demonstrate real insight into human behavior in particularly sensitive times. There is much to be learned from *Tough Talks in Tough Times*, but none more insightful than knowing when to be quiet. Jean has a great understanding into the human psyche during times when it is difficult to communicate.

D1446594

Joe Calloway
Author of Becoming A Category of One

Jean Palmer Heck delivers a straightforward, honest reality check in her new book, *Tough Talks in Tough Times*. Jean's five-step CHECK system for delivering tough talks is invaluable, not just to managers, but to anyone who ever faces challenging conversations (and that's all of us). This book provides real world strategies to effectively handle the toughest real world situations. A great book!

Dale Collie
Former U.S. Army Ranger and Fortune 500 Executive
Author of Winning Under Fire

Tough Talks in Tough Times should be on the desk of every manager. The tough talks are inevitable and you need to know how to deal with the topic and the person. One of the biggest mistakes made by leaders at all levels is that of putting off the talk that must happen eventually. Get a copy for yourself and one for the leader you're mentoring.

Doug Williams
President, Venture Logistics

After experiencing our organization's first downsizing in 17 years, this book takes on a special meaning for me. *Tough Talks in Tough Times* provides a clear and concise roadmap for addressing co-workers in a difficult time. This is definitely a valuable book for all business owners and their management staffs.

Steve Bluestein
Executive Vice President, Oscar Winski Co. Inc.

Jean Palmer Heck's *Tough Talks in Tough Times* is essential reading for anyone managing in today's business environment. It provides a roadmap for one of the more difficult aspects of managing, which is communicating effectively with your employees whether the news is good or bad. I'm confident that the use of her strategies will pay great dividends.

Tough Talks in Tough Times

What Bosses Need to Know to Deliver Bad News, Motivate Employees & Stay Sane

by Jean Palmer Heck

Higashi Publishing

Published by Higashi Publishing

Published in the United States of America

10 9 8 7 6 5 4 3 2 1

Heck, Jean Palmer
Tough Talks in Tough Times: What Bosses Need to Know to Deliver Bad News, Motivate Employees, and Stay Sane / by Jean Palmer Heck

ISBN: 978-0-9826167-0-3

Cover Design and Illustrations by Meta4 Design
Author's photo by Velse Photography
Printed in the United States of America

Tough Talks℠ and CHECK℠ are service marks of Real-Impact Inc.
All rights reserved.

Mixed Sources
Product group from well-managed forests and other controlled sources
www.fsc.org Cert no. SW-COC-002283
© 1996 Forest Stewardship Council

FSC

Higashi Publishing books are available at special quantity discounts for use as premiums and sales promotions or for use in corporate training. Special editions, including personalized covers and excerpts of the book, can be created by Higashi Publishing. For more information, contact: specialsales@higashipublishing.com.

To Gary, without whom this mission would never have been accomplished.

To Tim and Laura, who bring more joy than a mother can bear.

To Mom, who gives and gives and gives.

To Dad, who always told me I could accomplish anything.

Table of Contents

Table of Contents (cont.)

Table of Contents (cont.)

O h, if only I would have said…" How many times has that crossed your mind after you had a discussion with someone over a difficult topic? Whether it's a tough talk with co-workers, spouses, doctors, lawyers, teachers, parents, neighbors, or acquaintances, most people on both sides of the difficult conversation walk away wishing they had handled it differently.

Throughout my 30-year corporate career, I sat on both sides of the table during painful discussions. Each one would have benefited from the experiences and tips shared in the following pages. During my time at four Fortune 500 companies, I was privileged to be privy to the difficult conversations that impact every company, large or small. As a husband, father, neighbor, friend, and sometimes adversary, I have faced the same kind of tough talks that many of you have experienced.

So when Jean Palmer Heck told me she was writing a book and speaking at conferences about *Tough Talks in Tough Times*, I offered to help. I knew her work and was confident this book would make a significant contribution to existing literature about workplace communications. As the book progressed, it became evident that her Tough Talks CHECK system also applies to the tough talks in our personal lives.

I have enjoyed being a supporting cast member in the creation of this book. Jean has methodically pulled together an informative and entertaining page-turner of a self-help book that shares insightful personal stories. Being naturally inquisitive, she interviewed people from many industries and discovered stories, both business and personal, that are perfect examples from which to learn. The result is this compelling, easy-to-read book. I wish I had read it before embarking on the many tough talks I've suffered through over the past four decades.

Trying tough talks throughout my career

During our initial conversation about this book, one example after another flowed through my mind. One dated from my first corporate management position at Eli Lilly in the late 1970s. I was directed by my boss to talk with a female employee who routinely wore a non-conformist wardrobe — a.k.a. Maoist casual. With no previous training or guidance, I turned to the only book available at the time that I thought would help with the discussion — John Malloy's *Dress for Success*.

As we sat in my 8' x 10' cubicle, I nervously told the 23-year-old business school graduate, "Some people are complaining about your unconventional attire." As her face reddened (as did mine), I awkwardly pushed Malloy's book toward her and dug a deeper hole when I said, "Just look around you. The people who are succeeding in this company are dressing more appropriately than you. Perhaps this book can help you." She left my office in tears and left the company shortly afterward. I still have that copy of Malloy's book as a constant reminder of the importance to be prepared for difficult discussions. Business Tough Talk #1 Grade: D-minus. The mere fact that I got through it was the only reason I didn't give myself an F.

Even with having Malloy's book as a talisman, I continued to experience mixed results in tough discussions. At Sara Lee, I had to fire a direct report who was consistently late, failed to complete basic work assignments, and appeared to have odd, chemically-induced mood swings. We had a terrible, emotionally charged conversation. Even though the firing was totally justi-fied, I later almost wanted to apologize to him and start the termination discussion over again.

In 1993, I joined Sears, Roebuck and Co. and began building a world-class communications team as the company was reinventing itself. Unfortunately, economic and trend issues struck the company in the mid 1990s, forcing us to make significant staff reductions. Having grown fond of most members of my team, I spent many sleepless nights worrying about firing close friends. Among them was Dan Fapp, a 36-year veteran of the company.

I called Dan into the conference room adjacent to my office on the concourse level of the impressive new Sears headquarters, and painfully began the discussion. Being a veteran of our turbulent company, Dan knew immediately what was happening. Before I could finish my human resource-required termination monologue, Dan surprised me by saying, "Hold on a minute, Ron. You've got a deal." Dan had already done the mental arithmetic as soon as I mentioned providing two weeks of severance for every year worked. Dan quickly realized he could afford to stop working, but would now get paid for the period he had already planned to remain with the company before retiring. It was the only time I recall getting a hug from someone following a termination conversation.

Although I am personally thankful for the outcome of this particular discussion, I still didn't feel adequately prepared for this talk or the many others that followed.

In search of open, honest discussions

From the other side, I've worked for bosses who were not clear in their discussions with me. One CEO couched his corrective remarks in terms of buckets. During good performance reviews, he would tell me that my bucket was full, but during stressful times within the company, he would say the bucket was only half full or nearing empty. His discussions entailed multiple buckets, which became confusing. His direct reports would openly discuss their bucket status with amusement, still realizing that "below half full" meant their current employment would soon "kick the bucket."

Others, such as my wife, Sandra Culp, don't rely on metaphors to convey their points of view. My two sons, our two West Highland terriers, and anyone who knows Sandra would attest that she consistently provides clear, direct feedback. In today's sometimes touchy-feely world, straight talk can be startling, especially for those having second thoughts about their self-confidence or their actions. I can declare that open, honest discussions build lasting, trusting relationships—as evidenced from our 38 years of marriage. A psychologist friend of ours thought we were abnormal since we could only recall one major argument in our lives together. (For a while, I contended it wasn't a real argument, but she effectively quashed that claim by noting that I sent her flowers afterward.) She has mastered the art of delivering tough talks; I'm still working on it.

A history of adding value

Why did I believe, when I first heard about this book, that it would be a valuable resource? Because of my experience working with the author.

I first met Jean 30 years ago when she walked into my office at Eli Lilly to be interviewed for a media relations job opening. At that time, Jean was a local television news reporter and week-end anchor for WTHR-TV in Indianapolis. Even back then, she broke through the clutter. This was the first time I had ever seen a video resume, which I watched before my initial meeting with her. She ended her introduction by visually handing her résumé toward the camera. Everyone at Lilly who saw this knew Jean could communicate effectively.

During her Lilly career, Jean assumed increasing responsibilities as she became recognized for her ability to engage colleagues and employees through her clear, open communications style. Following her stint in media relations, Jean was promoted to head up global employee communications.

Perhaps based on her news reporting background, Jean always asked good questions and continued asking them until she got all the relevant information. Just as her firm's name, Real-Impact, implies Jean, indeed, has had a real impact on many lives, and this book will be able to help many more.

My initial gut reaction was right. If you are a manager who has experienced tough talks yourself, you will find much to relate to in this book. If you're just embarking on that phase of your career when you will no doubt find yourself facing difficult conversations, the following pages provide valuable insights and counsel from professionals who have had their fair share of tough talks.

Reading this book and applying its principles will make your tough talks a little easier.

E. Ronald Culp

Public relations veteran Ron Culp is a member of the PR News Hall of Fame and has received the Distinguished Service Award from the prestigious Arthur W. Page Society. Following a 30-year career that included senior communications positions at four major corporations, Ron is now partner and managing director at Ketchum, where he heads the agency's North America Corporate Practice.

Introduction

When was the last time you took a ride on a roller coaster—the kind that starts off in a tunnel? Do you remember what it felt like to see total darkness ahead of you and around you? How long would you climb the steep slope? Would you fall off? When would you plunge down? And when would it finally end? All parts of the ride sent danger signals to your head, your heart and your stomach.

I sat next to a colleague at a professional association meeting a few months ago and noticed that he had the look of someone who was on that roller coaster ride. His demeanor had the telltale signs of a person who only bought the ticket, stood in line, got on and strapped in because he was forced to: the furrowed brow, the tight lips, the uneven breathing.

When I asked this usually upbeat person what was wrong, he told me he just experienced one of his worst days ever. He had to deliver bad news to six people and would be facing the same thing later in the week. The recipients of the bad news were people he had come to know, respect, and like.

Then he posed a few rhetorical questions: Why wasn't there some kind of plan or system or book that would make that part of his job less traumatic? Why couldn't he gain the insights of people who had faced the same task? What would their advice be? What mistakes had they made and how could he avoid them?

And then he turned and asked me, "Why don't you write a book like that and speak about the tough talks that everyone has to give?"

My reaction was immediate: "I really hate conflict. Why am I the person who should write and speak about this?"

My colleague reminded me that my whole career had dealt with communications, many of them contentious. I was a spokesperson on controversial issues in the pharmaceutical industry, where plaintiffs' attorneys had primed the pump, arming news reporters with negative and biased "facts" on hot issues. I had worked with top-level executives at companies of all sizes, from the Fortune 100 to five-employee shops, strategizing important communications on tough topics. I've evaluated hundreds of speakers, often being hired by bosses who thought an employee needed help — even when the employee had no clue it was a career maker or breaker.

I had faced my own personal tough talks, as a giver and receiver: dealing with elderly parents who needed to give up driving; facing news of a failed relationship; and serving on nonprofit boards where key players had to be told to take a back seat.

Probably, the earliest sign that this book was in my future was the fact that I was the youngest of three children and thus many times the recipient of tough talks from older siblings who were smarter. Or at least a lot bigger.

In other words, I intimately experienced tough talks.

The purpose of this book is to share insights from people just like you who have received and given tough talks, primarily for business, but also in personal situations.

Professionals from all walks of life and all ages, including three psychotherapists, an employment attorney, a communications director at a major corporation, several human resource specialists, leaders in the field of corporate communications, small business owners, a professional athlete, and a musician have told me their stories. These people have shared the good, the bad, and the ugly. They've revealed their innermost thoughts and have opened up their hearts and souls to me, and thus, to you.

In most cases I have been able to use their names and details about their companies. However, there are a few times when the names and locations have been changed to protect those who have been in dangerous situations as a result of giving the tough talk. Rest assured, every story and case study in this book is true.

After researching the subject with hundreds of people who've given accounts of their tough talks, many still reeling with emotion, I've narrowed them down to 22 case studies and a five-step process for you to use with your next tough talk.

What this book is NOT:

- An exposé of companies or industries that have fired people, laid them off, or cut their salaries
- Stories of disgruntled employees
- A legal or psychology primer

What this book IS:

- Tough talks that worked
- Tough talks that did not work
- The impact of the tough talks on bosses
- The impact of tough talks on employees
- Insights into tough talks in life and death and war
- Stories involving drugs, sports, and rock 'n' roll
- Tear-jerking examples of lives that are coming to an end
- Uplifting stories of relationships, in and out of business, that have been healed by tough talks
- Lessons on surviving the aftermath of a tough talk
- Information on motivating the remaining workforce
- A process to follow for your next tough talk

Who should read this book?

This book is for you if you are a manager, a business owner, or a person who wants to advance in your career. Although the primary focus is on business, this book also has information that can be applied to tough talks in one's personal life.

Chapter 1 is an overview of tough talks, with discussions of the impact of instant communications, issues with different size companies, generational differences, and family concerns.

Chapter 2 focuses on what to do before the tough talk, how rumors affect productivity, self tough talks, preparation and advice about vulnerable employees. An employment lawyer chimes in with her observations.

Chapter 3 will highlight the tough talk itself, detailing a five-step process, the CHECK system, to use with your next difficult conversation.

Chapter 4 is about motivating the employees who remain after a layoff, plant closing, salary cut, or acquisition.

Chapter 5 is all about you. How you react to being the giver of bad news, dealing with stress, a self-care plan, and a look at your marketability are the topics of this chapter.

Chapter 6 has sound bites from the interviews I've conducted. They were too good to keep to myself. And because one of my areas of expertise is developing sound bites that people remember, I could not see these sage quotations go to waste.

Each chapter begins with a preview of what you will read in that chapter and ends with the major takeaways.

Finally, there is an appendix of resources for your use.

To keep your reading of this book easier, I have alternated the use of singular pronouns between masculine and feminine. Chapter 1 uses he and him, Chapter 2 she and her, etc.

This has been a tremendous growth experience for me as I've researched and written the book. I have learned from every person. I want to learn from you, too. Send me your thoughts at jean@toughtalks.biz or post on my blog, www.toughtalks.biz. Share your insights and examples with me and other readers. Ask questions. Become a tough talk expert. It's needed in these tough times. We'll get through them together.

Jean Palmer Heck

Chapter 1   Squeezed & Torn

In this chapter	
	• *Everyday tough talks*
	• *The emotional challenge*
	• *Impact of the media*
	• *Surviving a layoff*
	• *The empathy trap*
	• *Employee engagement*
	• *Integrity, loyalty & communication*

Natalie Wilson was tossing and turning in her bed at three o'clock on a cold mid-January morning. In fact, she had been so concerned about the financial results of the recent holiday season that she had not slept well since the new year began. Sales in Campus Classics, the custom-design apparel company she and her husband, Byron, had started 20 years before, had slumped by 15%. They had squeezed as much out of the budget as they could. But it was not enough. That meant one thing: their 25-person staff would have to shrink.

Natalie had already decided which three people would be let go, but she dreaded telling them. Respected by her staff as a caring, fair-minded, and even-tempered boss, she kept going over this nagging question in her mind: "Was there anything I could have done differently to prevent this layoff?"

Over the past two decades, revenue at the Wilsons' company had climbed steadily; net profit rose consistently; and life had fared well for the employees as well as the owners. While Byron was the visionary, Natalie was the one who made sure the details were executed, the operations ran smoothly, and the employees were productive. Although they had faced the typical obstacles that any company does, large and small, Natalie had always handled the issues well, solving them in her usual manner, with warmth and respect for her employees.

Natalie thought she had done all the right things. But this time, the economic downturn that had forced the company to cut staff had swelled feelings of self-doubt in her. Now, Natalie had to deliver bad news, the kind that puts those receiving the information on a totally unexpected track. It was a tough talk that she had not been prepared to deliver, but deliver it she must. When? How? What if...?

This debate kept playing out in her mind, even in the early hours of that winter morning.

Challenges beyond money

Natalie is among the hundreds of thousands of bosses squeezed by the economy and emotionally torn over the need to deliver bad news to employees. While the details of this strife may differ from one person to another and from one organization to the next, there are many more similarities than differences.

Tough talks are no fun for anyone other than the most sadistic people. In fact, tough talks are painful—both for those who receive the bad news and those who have to give it. They can cause stomachs to churn, heads to throb, and hearts to feel heavy.

Today's economic conditions are taking management to a whole new level of challenge and difficulty, affecting more than the dollars in our 401(k)s or the net value of our homes. Tough times impact our very psyches. And the tough talks that go with tough times—whether in business or in our personal lives—can seem unbearable.

Everyday tough talks

The angst that goes along with the tough talks is not reserved for the workplace alone. The anticipation, delivery, reactions, aftermath, and lasting emotions apply to tough talks in all aspects of life.

Think about the kinds of difficult conversations that must occur:
• A son has to take away his father's car keys and tell him it is time he moves into a retirement home.
• A department manager has to squelch rumors of a plant shutdown yet boost productivity to ensure it will not happen.

• A spouse has to tell a mate of 17 years their marriage is over.

• A newly named director has to inform staff members that their jobs are being outsourced to another country.

• A doctor has to explain to a patient that the cancer is incurable.

• A company owner has to find a way to make employees care about their appearance.

• A homeowner has to confront a neighbor about noisy teenage parties.

• A boss has to improve customer service quickly.

How you handle tough talks as a manager, owner, "hatchet man," spouse, adult child, or doctor will dramatically change lives.

The spotlight is on... you

When a tough talk gets delivered in the workplace, everybody is watching. Regardless of whether you are an introvert or an extrovert, as the boss you are in the spotlight. How you handle the situation will be observed and analyzed by more people than Monday morning quarterbacks after the Super Bowl.

If you assume that your actions in an individual employee situation are a private matter, you are kidding yourself. Be assured the other employees in the area are taking note. They want to know that the employee who is not productive has been held to the same standards they are. They want the situation resolved as much as you do. Act too soon, though, and the individual's best interests may be forgotten because important details may not be revealed; resolve it too late and those in the rest of the office, department, or company will suffer because of the lack of resolution.

Act too soon and the individual may suffer. Act too late and the company may suffer.

Some of those watching the drama play itself out want you to succeed; others hope you fail. Everything you do as a person of authority gets put under the microscope. Your employees will presume that whatever action you take or words you use with one individual will also apply to them. Your peers will watch to see if they can do it better. Your bosses will quickly assess your ability to handle other tough situations.

Face the elephants in the room

Then there is the trap of ignoring bad news, hoping it will go away or resolve itself. In the absence of information, rumors will always fill the vacuum. And if you do not face the elephants in the room, the pachyderms will trumpet the sounds of the discontented.

Their noise is compounded by the omnipresence of social media. Because video cell phones can post to YouTube almost instantly, your business has become radically transparent, whether you like it or not. Although critics say that technology has caused people to be less connected emotionally, when news of any ilk happens, these digital links, such as blogs, text messages, and tweets, heat up their passions at the speed of a mouse click.

If a company takes too long to communicate with employees, it does not mean that the question *What's going on?* will not be asked. It just means that it will be answered without your input. And that could be disastrous. Tough or not, it pays to keep talking.

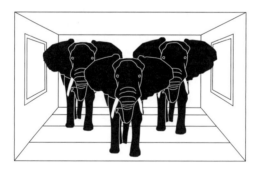

No story too tiny to report

As important as communication is with employees, the media play a significant role that should not be dismissed — by even the smallest operation. No story is too tiny to report. Nor is any organization too small to be burned by the ramifications of negative coverage.

Pick up your local newspaper (if it still exists) and notice how often it ties national news to the average person in your home-town. Reporters seek out local people to interview. They use that technique to make stories more relevant to their audiences. And bad news will always be fodder for the media.

Imagine your former employee standing in the unemployment line, telling a reporter that your company had no concern for its employees. Or that you put profit ahead of people. Or that you delivered the bad news in an e-mail.

Unfortunately, many companies, large and small, fail to develop relationships with the media during good times. In tough times, struggling organizations are getting plenty of media attention. Public perceptions seriously impact the morale of your employees, as well as your own stress levels.

Combine the plethora of news outlets, the explosion of social media, the rise in citizen journalism, and the global reach of the Internet, and you should be concerned with the message that is going out about your company. Do you have a plan to deal with the newshounds of today? If you do not, you would be wise to come up with one.

Source of sleepless nights

Dealing with the media and delivering bad news to groups of people will bring any anxiety about public speaking to the fore-front, especially if you feel uncomfortable with the information. Your stress level increases when you are not clear about the message. It bumps up again if your announcement means people will lose their jobs. And the intensity of your emotions may skyrocket if you fear pushback from your audience.

The tough talk that worries people most often, however, is the one that is delivered one-on-one. Just thinking about facing the person to whom you have to deliver the bad news can cause sleepless nights, as Natalie Wilson can attest.

If you consider yourself a kind person and assume that this bad news will devastate the receiver, then delivering it will be exceptionally unpleasant for you. Tough talks delivered in tough times by nice people have a way of crushing the spirit of the sender.

When empathy becomes a trap

EAPs can help workers cope with personal issues.

One trap that managers can fall into results from being empathetic. This is especially true for tough talks about an employee's performance. When a manager learns of a home situation that places stress on a particular employee, it can be hard to discipline that person. So the manager often puts it off or gives in, but eventually, if work performance does not improve, the manager can become a victim of the situation — often a resentful one.

Issues at home can certainly affect performance at work. To help with situations like these, large corporations contract with independent employee assistance programs, known as EAPs. These professional, confidential, outside counseling services, paid for by the company, help the worker cope with various personal issues so that the boss and employee can focus on reviving productivity on the job front.

Patti Ayars, a transformational change expert, explains EAP services using this example: "The employee shares with his manager that life at home is tough. The person might say, 'My elderly mother just broke her hip and my wife is in a serious depression. I know that my performance at work has been impacted; however, I don't have a choice. I have to take care of the problems at home.'

"In a case like this, the manager should not assume the role of therapist. This would be an ideal time to suggest the employee make use of the EAP benefit," she advises.

Destined to give tough talks

Niceness and EAPs aside, some bosses seem destined to be the bearer of bad news. They are the ones who manage employees who are not productive or those whose skills are not a correct match with the company or job.

The following story is a case study of one such manager who had a long career in a large corporation. Serving in a multitude of assignments, he had experience with many employee issues. His story, like all the others in this book, is true.

In most of the case studies throughout the book, I have been able to use the names of the people interviewed as well as the company or organization. In a few of the case studies, like the one on the next page, only first names have been used, sometimes pseudonyms, at the request of the interviewees. No matter what their preference, all the people interviewed for this book have made a huge difference in the lives of their employees. Thus, I call these case studies Real-Impact stories.

Real-IMPACT

Tough Talk Problem
Dealing with a career path not chosen

Interviewee
Paul S., a 50-year-old manager

Organization
A Fortune 100 company

Fifty-year old Paul S. is a man who enjoys sports, particularly the ones involving his college alma mater. He is known for razzing friends from competing schools every time they met, especially if his team has just won the most recent match.

For the 20-year employee of a Fortune 100 company, games are a pleasurable part of life — as long as they are on the sports field. But about six years ago, Paul saw a common game being played at work under the coaching of the human resource department that was not any fun.

The lower-case *p* on the personnel file had two meanings.

"I called it the little p game," said Paul, referring to the letter p that metaphorically went in front of someone's name in his employment file. It meant 'problem person.' It also meant 'Let Paul handle the problem.'

"The first time I had to fire someone, I was worried I might screw up," he admits. "I was nervous, knowing it was very easy to do or say the wrong thing that would make the situation worse and give the person a legitimate complaint about the company.

"I remember being concerned how I would handle it," he says. "I know that sounds selfish, but I was looking out for myself.

"I never had to terminate someone who was a jerk. In some cases, I had to terminate people that I really liked, but that's a part of corporate life.

"After several years, it dawned on me that I was managing an inordinate number of unproductive employees who had to be fired. I began to feel resentful, because I had become the resident 'hatchet man.' I figured out why: it was because when I asked people to leave, there were no negative ramifications."

As a result, Paul ended up managing numerous people whom the company considered marginal workers, but were given one more chance. "The company actually hoped they would leave. When it didn't work out that way, I had to fire them."

Paul finally told senior management that he did not appreciate the role he was forced into. "Those termination discussions were difficult, but the lessons I learned from going through the scenario many times has left me prepared for giving all sorts of tough talks."

Takeaway

Being able to deliver tough talks effectively is a skill that is valued by upper management. Although most bosses would prefer not to give them, they are an essential part of managing in these tough times.

Squeezed & Torn (cont.)

The silver lining of tough talks

There is an upside to delivering tough talks at work. How you handle employees can be a feather in your cap professionally; after all, performance management is a key skill that companies look at when they are hiring or firing.

Organizations value those who know how to deal with the employee who comes in late, the person who disrupts the work environment, and the worker who is not self-motivated. Likewise, having the ability to manage creative people, analytical folks, unstructured workers, highly organized employees, and star performers — the gamut of personalities — adds to a manager's internal marketability. Being adept at tough talks with all types of employees is an important part of performance management.

Receiving bad news

Don't assume the receiver hears the message you send.

The most important job you have as a boss is to communicate. The way you deliver information is only a portion of the whole communication process. The person or persons who are receiving the information also play a critical role. No matter what you say, write, draw, sign, translate, advertise, promote, video, tweet, or blog, what your audience takes away cannot be assumed. Unfortunately, many of us fail to remember that — at home and at work.

It is important to think about the recipients when you are preparing and delivering your tough talk. What will be their take on your message? How will they react? Much will depend on what the bad news is and their ability or inability to adapt. Their financial resources, their support networks, and their philosophies of life, among other things, play a role. In any case, they will experience a physiological and emotional jolt.

Because this is so important to consider, I asked everyone who was interviewed for this book — the people who had wonderful insights about how to deliver bad news — to recall what it was like when they were recipients of tough talks. What was done correctly and what was poorly handled? They generously shared their memories. The following is a case study that reflects one person's memories of a layoff at his company.

Tough Talk Problem
Surviving a layoff

Interviewee
Ron Kirkpatrick

Everybody liked it when the beer guy came around. It was the perfect job for Ron Kirkpatrick, the media relations director and West Coast face of Coors Brewing Company. He lived where he wanted and traveled enough to make it interesting, but not enough for it to be a burden on his family.

Ron had a great working relationship with his boss and enjoyed high-visibility experiences—like the time he adamantly advised Peter Coors about a need to rebuild the company's image in Los Angeles. There, certain retailers were taking the beer off their shelves and placing the cases in the gutter as a sign of their animosity toward the brewer. Having this kind of tough talk with the head of a company could either catapult a public relations career to a Rocky Mountain high or sink it to a Pacific Ocean low. Ron survived it, and eventually was promoted to community relations director.

As the company sought to grow, it began streamlining its operations and workforce, which meant layoffs. Ron survived the first round of downsizing. Six months later came the second reduction in force, or RIF. Then he got the call that took his own internal organs from the top of the mountain to the depths of the sea.

"I'm not hearing this. It can't be true," he thought as his boss of 12 years told him his position had been eliminated. "They can't mean me. I've been doing a good job out here in California. Surely they want to keep me here."

At first, Ron had five or six job possibilities outside of Coors. Comforted by the thought of his marketability, he decided to take a few days off from his job search to mentally regroup. Within that week, all his opportunities disappeared. That meant going back to the drawing board. It was tough for Ron, the only breadwinner in the family, to find employment. The reality hit him like a ton of bricks. "I hadn't done a good job of keeping up contacts in the marketplace," he says.

That cold strech, especially after the severance money ended, taught me a lesson: no one is ever safe from losing a job.

Ron had a strong resume. He had worked as a reporter, in a public relations agency, and in the corporate world. But the blow to his ego surprised even him. "The longer you go without a job, the more you doubt yourself," he reflects. "And it's very easy to get bitter. I still don't have fond thoughts of that time in my career, but I am respectful of Coors, its good product, and the fact that I learned a lot there."

While out of the workforce, Ron motivated himself by listening to certain songs, particularly "Sansei" by Hiroshima and "Changes" by David Bowie. He began meditating, reading positive books and affirmative adages, and avoiding negative people. After several months without income, Ron's wife, who had been a stay-at-home mom for ten years, started looking for a position in her area of expertise, which was education.

"That cold stretch, especially after the severance money ended, taught me a lesson: No one is ever safe from losing a job. You're only as good as your most recent performance, or as good as the company's last quarter. So you need to keep networking and growing your contact base."

One saving grace during Ron's time away from his career was being able to build a stronger relationship with his ten-year-old son, Grant, who appreciated having Dad coach his sports teams. Grant knew his father had financial worries and even offered to forego his allowance until Dad got a job.

In today's environment, it is a lot more palatable to be out of work due to market forces than to be let go because of a company's single-minded focus on its bottom line. "Innately, most of us understand the whole profit thing," Ron concludes, "except when someone cuts our job."

Takeaway

Even if your current job seems secure, change is inescapable. Put measures in place that make you marketable and employable. And keep in touch with the contacts in your network of business associates.

Not a unique story—even for small companies

A company's size has a huge effect on tough talks.

Unfortunately, the Real-Impact story about Ron is not unique. There is hardly a street in any town where someone has not lost his job. Nor is there a boss who has not delivered a tough talk in the form of a layoff, a termination, a salary cut, or a performance review.

A company's size has a huge effect on tough talks. It may seem easier for a small company owner or manager to ad lib a difficult conversation, especially with employees who feel like family members (and who actually might be blood relatives or extended family). But that is bad business practice. The same preparation required for a tough talk with employees in large corporations is needed in medium and small companies, too.

Management professor Peter Cappelli, of the Wharton School of the University of Pennsylvania, writes about it this way: "Layoffs are more complicated for small- and mid-sized companies than for larger enterprises. For smaller companies, the process is more personal—and thus painful—and often there are few or no [human resource] specialists to help out. The temptation is to just 'wing it' and move on. But that is one of the biggest mistakes smaller firms make because it creates misunderstandings that can lead to unnecessary clashes."[1]

If your company is small, the mere fact that you are working with people who may be your best friends does not excuse you from well-thought-out preparation for any kind of difficult discussion. Even though you work together—and maybe play together—for 40 to 50 to 60 hours a week, you still must deliver tough talks as the consummate professional you are so that no one misconstrues the message.

What happens when you are faced with situations in which you have no experience? The next Real-Impact story reveals how one young boss fared.

Tough Talk Problem
Letting people go when you're the new boss

Interviewee
Rose Gailey

Organization
An elementary school, Texas

"Firing discussions are never easy," says Rose Gailey, who early in her career found herself in a situation where her tough talks would be directed at employees several years her senior.

When Rose was in graduate school, she began teaching at a local private elementary school as a bridge to her future career. While teaching, she began to support the administration. Within a very short time she was named principal of a 500-student elementary school. All by the ripe old age of 23!

As principal, Rose faced a significant management challenge with two teachers. One was always late, leaving the kids stranded outside while other children were already in the class-rooms; the other became more of a pal with the students rather than their educator.

She had tried to confront the problem and set clear parameters with both teachers, but the issues did not disappear. "There was no way we could go through another school year with either of them," Rose recalls.

The young principal did not have a game plan to follow for this situation; however, she did not morally feel she could just let them go without helping them find other work. She looked at their performance. If not in this job setting, where could they be successful?

"I knew I couldn't renew their contracts," says Rose, "but I didn't want to do that without a plan for their transition. I felt it should be turned it into something positive. In essence, I was a principal, a counselor, and an outplacement agency at the same time."

What was the lesson this young school principal learned? "I can't 'fix' others. I can only guide them," says Rose. "They make choices in their lives, not me. If I carry the ball and never give them accountability, then I'm letting them down. If I've got the ball and throw it to them, they can catch it and run with it. They have to be empowered to make any changes themselves."

When Rose saw one teacher 20 years later, the woman thanked her for getting her out of teaching. "She was in the marketing field and loving it. And very successful at that."

Takeaway **The boss is not in control of a worker's fate; the employee is.**

Learning the ropes

Like Rose, I, too, was placed in a management position early in my career. None of my schooling or on-the-job experience readied me to be the boss of a staff made up of employees 15 to 25 years my senior. Despite internal training classes with other new supervisors, I was woefully unprepared for my first management position.

The transition from being a television news anchor to a corporate spokesperson in a pharmaceutical company had been a delightful challenge for me. I was no stranger to getting information from top-level executives. Having previously interviewed the president of the United States, the first man to walk on the moon, and even the "Corn King" of Indiana's State Fair, I had no qualms about going to the executive floor and working with senior people to craft the company's message on tough topics. The fact that I was not a research scientist or pharmacist did not faze me. I had not been an astronaut either, but that did not hinder my reporting skills.

Having done my media relations job well, I was promoted early in my career at Eli Lilly and Company to head up employee communications globally. I had staff members who knew much more about the company than this wet-behind-the-ears news junkie.

At the time, the company probably overestimated my ability to manage a staff and deliver tough talks during performance reviews. The mistakes I made as a young boss, still fresh in my memory, most likely did not have lasting effects on anyone except me. But times were more prosperous then compared to now — and much less litigious.

Mistakes made in management today by a young, or old, manager or business owner can have significant financial and legal ramifications for a company. And being unprepared to communicate bad news can lead to major misunderstandings.

Integrity, loyalty & communication

Your workforce is scared.

How the employees perceive the boss or business owner, no matter what the age, goes a long way in determining whether a tough talk in tough times is motivating, frightening, or somewhere in between.

Chances are your workforce is scared. And being scared by media hype or economic trends is one thing. Being frightened because company leaders do not communicate often enough or effectively is another. Remember, a key element in your job as boss is your ability to communicate.

The high cost associated with losing good workers because they go to other employers makes it essential that companies do what they can to engender loyalty. Current research shows that when the economy rebounds, a surprisingly large number of employees plan to seek new employment — 54%, according to Adecco, a recruiting and employment company. Compounding the problem for employers is that 71% of the highly sought-after Millennial generation, also known as Generation Y or Echo Boomers (those born in the 1980s and '90s), say they will leave.[2]

Essential discussions

Increase your communications in tough times — even if it is not comfortable.

Open, honest, two-way communication is always an essential practice to keep good employees. If you want your business to survive in tumultuous times, you must communicate more often and be straightforward in your everyday conversations. Make sure the people working for you understand how the business is faring in the current economic climate and what they can do to help improve it. They want to know that what they do, and how they do it, makes a contribution to the organization. And they need to hear it in your words.

It is important to give employees more than a paycheck. They want an honest assessment of their roles within the big, changing picture... and your support.

Follow the leader

Employees will judge your integrity.

The regard employees have for their leaders correlates to their commitment to the company. Employee loyalty is an area that has been measured frequently over the years by Walker Information. According to its research, only 57% of people surveyed felt senior leaders were people of high personal integrity.[3]

As Walker's senior consultant Chris Woolard says, "When the leaders with low integrity ratings discount those findings and say, 'My employees never interact with me. How would they know?' my response is 'That is the problem. If they don't know you, they can't know you have integrity.'"

Do your workers know in their heads and feel in their hearts that competent, caring human beings with integrity are making the decisions? That is a tough question to ask and an even tougher one to answer objectively. But you must be able to answer with a resounding Yes! Remember, the human factor goes a long way with employees.

Consider the next two Real-Impact stories. The personalities of the leaders have a direct bearing on the tone of the work environment. In the first case, the company and chief executive officer are named. In the second, pseudonyms are used.

Real-IMPACT

Tough Talk Problem
Closing manufacturing sites

Interviewee
Maril MacDonald

Organization
Pitman-Moore

Pitman-Moore was a veterinary pharmaceuticals and animal health products company that had grown rapidly through acquisitions until the market began to slow down in the 1980s. At that time, most of the big pharmaceutical companies had large agricultural divisions that produced competing products, eating up more and more of the market share. So CEO Bill Mercer found himself facing gut-wrenching decisions about which plants to close and how to inform the employees.

Bill could keep the decision process to himself and other top executives, while trying to contain the inevitable bad news until the last possible moment. Or he could face the masses and tell them exactly what he knew and what was still up in the air. Maril MacDonald, then vice president of communications for Pitman-Moore, joined Bill as he visited each plant. "We took the time to explain to the employees what was happening, what timetable they could expect for changes, and what was still being discussed. Bill gave his word that he, himself, would come back to lay out any final decisions when they had been made."

While adopting an open-book policy with the employees in tough times made the executive and the company vulnerable to security and safety issues, he found there was no bull's-eye on his back; he was not a target for their anger at all. Quite the contrary. In fact, Pitman-Moore's employees recognized that they were being treated fairly. "In turn, they showed Bill the respect he had earned by being open and honest," says Maril.

"Productivity at the plants that were being considered for closing didn't waver. In some cases, it even went up. And when Bill announced which plants would close or be sold, employees stayed with him to the very end."

Takeaway

Integrity in actions and constant communication trump rumors, fears, and dissension.

Squeezed & Torn (cont.)

 **Real-IMPACT**

Tough Talk Problem
The exploding boss

Organization
A 100-employee technology company

Max D. worked hard his entire life to build a reputation as a forward-thinking strategic player who executed his work responsibilities with quality and speed. He had taken all the necessary steps to move up the management ladder to a position of power in the company and prestige in the industry. On the surface, the 42-year-old general manager seemed to be a competent captain of the ship.

The owners of the company, located 200 miles away, believed all was smooth sailing. But if they had been present on a daily basis, rather than just showing up on pre-scheduled trips, they would have found a leader with the personality of the fictional Captain Queeg. And his serious control issues were taking a toll on the crew.

Max was convinced that no one could do a job as well as he could. As a result, he regularly swooped in, appropriated tasks, and embarrassed many employees in the process. When a member of his team brought up issues that needed to be ad-dressed, he would often blow up. As a result, Max's employees hesitated to discuss the mundane, yet necessary, tasks required for an effective operation.

His administrative assistant, Hanna M., one of the few people around Max who did not cower in his presence, developed a sig-nal to alert coworkers to Max's mood of the moment. An avid photographer, Hanna had a display of her own photos on her desk and her computer screen saver. When Max was in a foul mood, she displayed a photo of a storm at sea, signaling the need to speak cautiously. If he was in a good mood, a sailboat in clear waters appeared, indicating that a discussion with him should be safe. The sailboat photo frequently was docked in the bottom drawer of her desk.

Max was stretched thin like many managers today, yet he seldom trusted his employees to do anything without him. Increasingly, his team members harbored resentment at being treated with so little respect. They knew they could help improve efficiency if their boss would just let them.

Ironically, Max often complained that his team was letting him down. He knew that he should set specific expectations for his employees in less stressful situations, but he never seemed to have the time.

Consequently, work life had turned into a sea of misery for both Max and his employees — and the sale of over-the-counter antacids at the pharmacy down the street rose accordingly. The captain of this ship did not realize mutiny was a distinct possibility. His top performers disembarked as soon as they could find a safe harbor.

Takeaway **When the boss explodes, no one wins.**

Fear of the boss

Even when the job forecast is bleak, management by intimidation doesn't work.

Clearly, Bill Mercer's style engendered loyalty and increased productivity. Max depended on management by intimidation, which, if it did increase output, ensured that the results were only temporary.

Many young employees come into the workplace with respect for—bordering on fear of—their superiors, even if their bosses do not operate like Max. When they have to deliver bad news to a person of higher authority, they hesitate. Maybe they still relive experiences from their childhoods, remembering what it was like not to know the equation in algebra class. Maybe a lower-than-expected grade on their report card brought an "I'm-disappointed-in-you" discussion with Mom or Dad. In any case, some workers today are fearful of communicating with their bosses. This intensifies the need of bosses to communicate with young hires.

Several Generation Y professionals confided in me that their toughest talks were not about breakups with significant others but about quitting their jobs, asking for a raise, or seeking a promotion. They feared their bosses' reactions.

Encouraging employee engagement

Organizations that communicate how important their employees are to the company, while seeking and valuing the employees' opinions, tend to have a more motivated, productive workforce and a healthier bottom line than those that do not. In human resource vernacular, this is called "employee engagement."

Studies by Watson Wyatt, a global consulting firm specializing in human resources and financial issues, show that "employee engagement is a leading indicator of financial performance. Companies that take steps to improve engagement levels can expect to experience higher subsequent financial returns."[4]

More than a marriage

Exactly what does the term "employee engagement" mean? Ask your workers and they may think it has something to do with what happens before marriage. On the surface, it does not; but in essence, it is similar. Employee engagement is a union of the values and actions of the employer and the employee. But that's a lot of theory. In practice, employee engagement means:

• Employees are in the communications loop at all times.
• Every worker has a stake in the success of the company and knows it.
• Words from management are in sync with their actions.
• There are frequent, meaningful conversations with workers about the state of the business.
• There is an emotional connection to the mission of the organization.
• Employees understand—and are respected for—what their roles mean, collectively and individually, to the success of the company.
• Professional development and training takes place on a regular basis.
• Supervisors communicate up and down the chain and actively seek their employees' input on most aspects of the business.

The next Real-Impact story shows how one company engaged its employees and reaped the rewards.

Squeezed & Torn (cont.)

Tough Talk Problem
Empowering employees in tough times

Organization
Toyota Motor Sales U.S.A.

In the current desert-like economic environment, survival has been dependent on a return to the basics and innovative thinking by all companies, no matter what the size. One of the largest segments affected by the tough times is the automotive industry, which has required significant "irrigation" to improve bottom-line performance.

Take, for example, the case of Toyota Motor Sales, U.S.A., which was not able to pay merit increases in 2009 — something unheard of in the 50-plus years the company has been operating in the United States. One of the few car giants that did not file for bankruptcy, Toyota did not like what it was seeing in the marketplace. And it was important that all the employees be made aware.

It began in the fall of 2008, when financial forecasts were especially bleak. The company anticipated possible budget shortfalls and faced the possibility of losing money. Knowing that the state of the world economy was beyond their control, executives knew it was possible to cut budgets. And if all the employees put their heads together, perhaps even unexplored revenue ideas could be generated. Thus, GAME ON was born. GAME ON stands for Gain Advantage, Maximize Efficiencies, Overlook Nothing.

The idea behind GAME ON was that employees would not feel so powerless in this economy if they could take a thoughtful, active role in helping the company get through tough times. So they were encouraged to consider more than the traditional budget-cutting exercises. Anything and everything, as the theme suggests, was fair game for consideration.

"This goes back to our basis in Kaizen," the continuous improvement system known to have turned around productivity and Japanese manufacturing, explains Ron Kirkpatrick. Ron, the former Coors employee who now serves as Toyota's national manager of executive/internal communications and social media, adds, *"We do it naturally. But because we get busy in our everyday lives, it's easy to get out of the discipline of thinking and acting on the Kaizen principle. Specific actions have to be on our calendar."*

As a result, the company had set a start and stop date for the GAME ON program. Announced in January of 2009, each division was challenged to brainstorm problems. And brainstorm they did. By the end of June 2009, the employees had sent in more than 800 possible solutions.

The revenue-sharing GAME ON ideas included studying new geographical markets, with the commercial market for light trucks a particular area of focus. To handle the North American glut of Tundra and Sequoia models, someone suggested taking them to the Middle East. There, money still flowed like high-viscosity motor oil, and these stable, durable vehicles could survive the frequent dust storms.

"Historically, Toyota had talked for years about importing cars into the U.S. but thought that manufacturing cars in the States would be too expensive," Ron explains. *"But with an efficient production system now in place and ideally suited products, it made financial sense to go after the export market. So we did."*

Other cost-cutting suggestions included dropping programs that had outgrown their usefulness. For example, the bimonthly magazine for employees cost $45,000 a year. Concerns about the environment and cost efficiencies were answered by putting most internal messages online. Communications were not cut; in fact, they increased, but not with the delivery systems of the past.

Squeezed & Torn (cont.)

In the GAME ON cost-saving efforts, Toyota employees also envisioned job movement in which people in traditional but almost obsolete roles would be asked to move to new areas.

Additionally, office cleaning has been cut back from a nightly task to a few times a week, and computers and lights are being turned off when employees leave work. Even the petunias are being pruned less frequently.

The bottom line: A shift of an estimated $240 million has resulted from GAME ON suggestions.

Takeaway

Your employees are smart. Bring them into the solution.

The head, heart & voice factors

Many of the stories in this book demonstrate a tactical approach to the "head" side of leadership. It is important for employees to know where the business stands in today's tough times. And they must understand exactly what their roles are.

A mistake too many people make, no matter what size the company, is the tendency to shelter people from bad news. The thinking is that employees would become comatose if they knew what kept you, as owner or executive, up at night. But as the Toyota Real-Impact story shows, bringing workers in on the bad news can pay enormous rewards if they are allowed to be part of the solution.

The "heart" side of leadership is an equally important factor. As the Pitman-Moore story reveals, employees can stay loyal to the end if they know their leader has integrity and communicates with honesty and transparency.

And the importance of "voice"? As Natalie Wilson tells her employees, "Every issue comes down to communication. It's one of the toughest things about running a business, whether times are tough or not."

When you have to give a tough talk to an employee or group of workers, how do you prepare before the words come out of your mouth? The next chapter, *Dribble & Shoot*, will give you a lot to think about from people who have walked in your shoes.

Squeezed & Torn (cont.)

- Tough talks are painful—both for those who receive the bad news and those who have to give it.

- Tough times impact our very psyche.

- In the absence of information, rumors will always fill the vacuum.

- The anticipation, the delivery, the reactions, the aftermath, and the emotions apply to tough talks in all aspects of life.

- As a boss, you are in the spotlight.

- The media play a significant role that should not be dismissed by even the smallest operation.

- Employees understand profits and losses except when their own jobs are being cut.

- Tough times show the necessity of networking when times are good.

- Empathy can become a trap.

- Knowing how to deliver tough talks can actually be an asset to your career.

- How employees regard the integrity of their leader correlates to their commitment to the company.

- Integrity in actions and communications trumps rumors, fears, and dissension.

Mike Cutler heard a rumor that he was getting a promotion. The news director of KVBC-TV, the NBC affiliate in Las Vegas, Nevada, had just returned from a Radio-Television News Directors Association national conference when it began circulating. He was settling into his high-backed, black leather chair, taking note of what was being shown on the TV monitors nestled in the cherry cabinet across the room, and looking through his e-mails when he got a phone call from a buddy in Atlanta.

"Congratulations, Mike! I just read that you got promoted."

"If it happened today, it's news to me," quipped Mike, using a standard punch line in the journalism business. "Seriously, why do you say that?"

"I just read the article in *Shop Talk* [the trade daily for broadcast journalists] about your replacement and your new position with the station."

Mike quickly ended the call and went to see the station's general manager, who told him to sit down.

"I should have told you yesterday, but we have hired a new head of the news department, and you won't be needed here anymore." So much for the rumor of a promotion and new position. So much for a job.

Dribble & Shoot (cont.)

I'm not dissatisfied with you, but these things happen.

"I was blindsided," says Mike. "There are jobs where you know the relationship is not going well and that something could happen, such as being terminated. But in this case, I had been given no indication that my performance had slipped. Our station had been number one in ratings." The ratings are what advertising rates are based on, and thus, the profitability of the news division.

"I had a good relationship with the general manager," continued the Emmy Award winner. "But apparently not good enough."

"I had been there seven years and most news directors only last two. The general manager said a fresh news director could challenge the reporters with different ideas. And he had an opportunity to hire someone else, so he took it. He said, 'I'm not dissatisfied with you, but these things happen.'"

After a brief conversation about the five-month severance package that included the use of a company car, Mike returned to his office, stunned, called his wife, cleaned out his desk, passed through the busy newsroom, and drove home.

Later that fall, after two months without work, Mike was offered a job as assistant news director at WTVF in Nashville, Tennessee. Unfortunately, it was a step backward for less pay, so he turned it down. It was not until February of the next year, after several months with no income, that Mike decided he had to face reality and take the Nashville job for which he was overqualified.

"Because I wasn't news director, I had the feeling of not being good enough." Two years later, after being promoted to news director, Mike felt like himself again.

"In the end, it worked out great. I can say that WTVF is the most ethical and honest station in the business. I always knew where I stood with management, and my reporters and anchors always knew what I expected of them.

"I hired reporters to be aggressive and inquisitive—someone newsmakers would trust and want to communicate with. It is not a business that can be based on rumors. Communication has to be up front and direct."

"When someone wasn't up to our expectations, I made sure he or she knew it and received the help needed to improve." There were no rumors in Mike's newsroom. And tough talks were delivered when they were needed.

The rumor mill

Are parking lot pundits demoralizing your team?

If there is one business in which the rumor mill never stops, it has to be the business of professional sports. Just read any sports section or listen to sports talk radio, and by comparison you will think your place of business houses a dream team untouched by controversy.

Take the National Basketball Association as an example. If a team loses three games in one week, word gets out that the wheels are coming off the franchise, the coach is about to be fired, and your favorite guard will be selling used cars by the end of the month.

In mid-February, around the time of the NBA trade deadline, rumors resonate at an especially high pitch. "It was always a fearful time," says Mark Eaton, the 7'4" former Utah Jazz center who does not look like he could be afraid of anything. "In the NBA, once you were traded, you had 48 hours to get to the new city. I worried that I'd have to leave my family and live in a hotel for the rest of the season."

Athletes who are not performing well wind up on the end of the bench quickly. Players spending time far removed from the coach's ear can create problems, almost like being a cancerous growth on the team's spirit. They begin demeaning the coach, their teammates, and the franchise. "When they would start issuing their opinions to other players about various situations, we'd call them 'locker room lawyers,'" Mark recounts. "It was detrimental to the team's morale. Most coaches get rid of these kinds of guys as quickly as they can."

Dribble & Shoot (cont.)

Water cooler talk can sink a company.

The talk of doubt and fear about work instability plays like a favorite song on the iPod in a professional athlete's ear. That is also what echoes around the world in the current economic climate. Look around; locker room lawyers reside in your company's lunchroom, too. But one significant and obvious difference lies between the realities of professional athletes and the rest of us in the workforce: we do not have the luxury of being traded to another franchise or team. Consequently, rumors can be terrifying.

When circumstances result in job losses due to market forces, lousy management, or poor performance, it signifies another up-tick in the current unemployment statistics. The tick, tick, tick of the numbers changing on the business scoreboard becomes fodder for the news media throughout the day, week, month, and year.

How doubts turn into lost productivity

Doubts and rumors drag down productivity.

Doubts about the economy turn into fears; fears, into rumors; rumors, into mental paralysis; mental paralysis, into lost productivity. Lost productivity feeds on itself, leading again to doubts, fears, rumors, mental paralysis, and so on, like a never-ending spiral. It requires strong leaders and constant communication to offset the doomsday scenarios being played over and over in the minds of the employees and reported by the media.

Doubts
Fears
Rumors
Mental Paralysis
Lost Productivity

What are the locker room lawyers around the water coolers at your place of business espousing?
Are the break room big shots imparting doom and gloom analyses to their coworkers? Are the parking lot pundits demoralizing your team? If so, your tough talk may be long overdue.

Change: the core of every tough talk

Every tough talk has to do with a change in someone's life. For example, you may be telling a couple of workers that they have to change their attitudes and resolve a conflict or they will be fired. Your tough talk may convey information about changes in benefits and compensation. If rumors are rampant, you may have to change your own communication process in order to halt them.

On the personal side, ending a relationship or beginning a new phase of life certainly involves major change, often heartbreaking ones. Change necessitates communication, often a sticking point in any type of relationship.

Communicating change is a must

Lack of communication indicates a lack of trust.

"A lack of communication indicates a lack of trust," avows Mark Eaton, who now owns two highly Zagat-rated restaurants. "As a result, if your employees don't feel trusted and safe, there's no cooperation, collaboration, or innovation." Then their defense mechanisms take control.

Recently, Mark's business partner decided to retire. In the restaurant business, as in many fields, there are no secrets. So although nothing had been officially announced, the employees caught a whiff of an impending change, which was as disconcerting to them as the smell of overripe fruit.

When rumors began circulating about one of the partners retiring, a prospective owner started making frequent visits to popular Salt Lake City dining establishments, which added speculation to the "stew" of kitchen gossip.

"One of our biggest concerns," Mark says, "was that we'd lose our key employees and have to re-staff. To avoid that, we were proactive in keeping them in the communications loop, which gave them a sense of peace. We assured them we'd keep the same operation going and that the only changes to be made would involve upgrading."

Dribble & Shoot (cont.)

Anticipation is worse than the tough talk

Anxiety before the tough talk can be as harrowing as the tough talk itself.

Whether you must announce that jobs are being eliminated, a marriage is over, or there is no more money in savings, the emotions and symptoms you experience *before* the tough talk can be as harrowing as the conversation itself. Upset stomachs, headaches, muscular aches and pains, and toothaches from grinding teeth as well as sleeplessness, sleepiness, irritability, lack of concentration, and even acne commonly show up before a tough talk.

When our son, Tim, a lieutenant in the United States Marine Corps, came home on a ten-day leave before being deployed to Iraq, he told my husband and me on the first day that he needed to talk with us about some serious issues. It was a tough talk I did not want to hear, he did not want to give, and we all anticipated with dread. But instead of having it at the beginning of his stay, all three of us silently agreed to put it off until later.

When my son left for Iraq we had a tough talk I didn't want to hear, he didn't want to give, and one that we all dreaded.

On the surface, the days preceding the tough talk went well. Underneath, I was a wreck: my stomach was doing somersaults, my tensed-up shoulders hovered around my ears, and anyone trying to converse with me only got blank stares in return. Fortunately for my business associates, I had turned down all engagements, suspecting I would be less than productive. Truthfully, I was beyond less-than-productive; I was useless.

With most of our relatives coming for a weekend send-off party, you might think I could muster the mental strength to put together a menu and grocery list. Not so. Without my friends doing the complete planning, preparation, cooking, and setup, the Heck and Palmer contingents would have been eating delivery pizza and Chinese take-out.

Once our relatives left, the tough talk with our son could no longer be avoided. Our first-born—the pudgy, happy-go-lucky baby who was never permitted to play with toy guns—looked so tall, strong, and responsible as we sat at the kitchen table. I did not even bother to keep a stiff upper lip and hide my emotions. I set an entire box of Puffs in front of me and used most of

Once the relatives left, the tough talk could no longer be avoided.

them while Tim detailed what he wanted us to do for a funeral and burial in case he gave his life for our country in Iraq.

Oddly, I felt a sense of peace in the midst of this tough talk. The emotions wreaking havoc on every fiber of my being had been released. In fact, the pent-up anxiety *about* the tough talk was worse than the tough talk itself. It made the actual goodbye a few days later seem like a cakewalk.

Yes, I still cried, but I had enough composure to tell him how proud I was of what he was doing and what a great kid he had always been, topped off with, "For heaven's sake, don't be a hero!" His father said the same thing but used a few flavorful adjectives from his Navy days to emphasize his thoughts.

Delay of game

Anxiety and sleeplessness are driven by a lack of clarity and acceptance of what has to happen.

Procrastination. It is a fairly normal reaction to a difficult talk, says Deborah Del Vecchio-Scully, a licensed professional counselor. However, as our family's story shows, procrastination leads to more pressure, stress, and anxiety. Ultimately, it was more challenging than facing the pending tough talk head on. It is no different with a person's difficult discussions at work.

"The hardest part of a tough talk," Deborah points out, "is tolerating what you feel about the message you are communicating."

Rose Gailey, now an executive coach with Gagen MacDonald, a strategy execution firm, concurs, adding that it is even harder when the company has not solidified its message and plan of action. "Anxiety and sleeplessness are driven by lack of clarity and acceptance of what has to happen," she says.

"I've worked with caring leaders who rationally understand the tough message but struggle with it emotionally," says Rose. "Often it's based on the assumption that the person who gets the bad news will be devastated."

The deliverer of the tough talk may
• Be in a wait-and-hope-for-change mode
• Disagree with and possibly resist the decision
• Blame herself, thinking, "Could I have done something else to be in a different position?"

As Rose says, "Any clash or disconnect the company's actions have with the person's belief system compounds the emotional strain."

Another psychotherapist, Maria Pozo-Humphreys, a specialist in cross-cultural counseling, says it is important to realize that loss is part of life. "Leaders don't have a free pass on that.

"No matter how accomplished and competent the boss is, there can be a tremendous amount of angst that gets in the way of action being taken," she adds. "This can be especially gut-wrenching when the boss sees himself or herself as a kind and compassionate type of person."

Add the word "nurturing" to a person's core characteristics and it can compound the internal struggle. While that may not be a typical business school term, it does apply to many small business owners, as the next Real-Impact segment shows.

Real-IMPACT

Tough Talk Problem
Convincing yourself of the need for a tough talk

Interviewee
Natalie Wilson

Organization
Campus Classics

If she had to do it over, she would have had the tough talk earlier.

When I asked Natalie Wilson (the small business owner whose sleepless nights were shared in Chapter 1: Squeezed & Torn*) about her biggest challenge communicating bad news to her employees, she quickly answered, "First, the tough talk I had to have with myself."*

Employees knew that the holiday season at Campus Classics was not going well. "My embroidery manager for 11 years was acutely aware of the difference in workload," says Natalie. "She came to me and said, 'I'm hearing you're going to let the top salaried person in each department go to cut back on payroll.'"

Natalie assured her manager that the rumor being spread among the 25 full-time employees and five seasonal workers was not true. "But that's when I had to have the tough talk with myself. I had to admit I had hard decisions to make. There was a payroll problem and I had to do something about it."

Physically, she felt her heart racing and her body heating up even in the cold January weather. But those symptoms did not speed her tough talk along. "Once I calculated that three jobs would have to be eliminated, it took me three weeks to call the employees into my office. I wondered how much productivity was lost by my procrastination. Putting my head in the sand didn't help anything."

What did she do during those three weeks of lost sleep? "I had numerous self-talks trying to convince myself layoffs were the right thing. I had to finally realize my responsibility as owner is to do what's best for the company, not to nurture the employees or make everyone happy—like the people pleaser I am.

"Too many business owners look at workers like they are robots, but I have a personal relationship with each of them. I truly value them as people. Laying off three people was a horrible decision I had to make."

If she had to do it over, Natalie says she would have acted two weeks sooner. "I needed one week to gather information and pray over it," reflecting how she depends on her faith to influence her decision-making process at home and work. "I also needed to reacquaint myself with the paperwork: COBRA, health insurance forms, reminders to get the security keys, and so on. I had to make up my own checklist; there was no system in place for this situation."

Many who face tough talks at work do not leave the tension behind at the office. For Natalie, her husband, Byron, who usually works outside their facility, provided a good sounding board at home. She also told her adolescent children what was happening so they would understand her unusual behavior. "I was very easily distracted. It was hard to focus on what they were saying to me and respond accordingly."

When she finally told her employees of her decision, she was emotionally spent. "I was ready to go home but had to rally to make it through the day. I owed that to the other workers."

A few days later, after all was said and done, "I felt the weight lift off my shoulders. Why did I wait so long to tell them? It had to happen anyway."

Takeaway

Hoping the circumstances surrounding the tough times will change adds to procrastination and stress. It is best to move forward quickly once a decision has been made.

Tough Talk Problem
Mustering up the nerve to have a tough talk

Interviewee
Megan Johnson

Organization
Scale Model, a rock band

Do rock bands and corporations have similar issues as professional colleagues when it comes to severing relationships? Just because the clothing, hairstyles, body piercing, and tattoo standards—not to mention the working hours—are quite different, tough talks are just as hard.

Megan "Rox" Johnson is the lead singer, backup guitarist, and keyboard player for Scale Model, an indie rock band orginally based in Chicago. She and her husband of six years, guitarist Dave Johnson, started jamming with anyone eager to play their instrument on stage and eventually meshed with two other musicians to play the club circuit.

While Megan and Dave practiced by themselves any chance they could get, their bandmates were less structured. And Megan, who earned a master's degree in cultural and organizational communication, wanted to approach her passion with the same degree of discipline and structure that she used in her academic studies and her nine-to-five world.

"Dave and I decided we really wanted to make it big in the music world. The way to do that was getting out there, playing as many shows in as many different towns as possible."

And practice, practice, practice. As the old joke goes: A tourist in New York City asks a street musician, "How do you get to Carnegie Hall?" His answer: "Practice, man."

So Megan and Dave, not wanting to get to New York's Carnegie Hall but rather to headline at Chicago's Lollapalooza festival, thought their band should practice together at least three times a week. Their band mates were resisting. Resentments were building.

Dribble & Shoot (cont.)

Since both she and her husband hate confrontation, Megan knew their tough talk would not be easy. "So we sat down and told them together. We explained our goals and said if the others weren't on board, we would have to find people who were. They took it personally and said that, for them, our friendship was more important than our personal goals. They thought we should try to work it out."

But that was not to be the case. Megan explained in subsequent discussions that even in the case of working with best friends, they would still make the same decision. "A true friend would respect our dream," she said.

They eventually found a new drummer and bass player. One of the former band members still harbors resentment.

What was Megan's takeaway? "If I had to do again, I wouldn't have waited so long to have the discussion. We thought about it, and it was obvious that our friendship was dissolving for the five or six months that we let our disagreements continue. It got harder the longer we waited."

Takeaway **Resentments build when tough talks are put on hold. Do not procrastinate.**

Shooting from a distance

The word goodbye takes a piece of your soul, too.

Preparing for a tough talk boils down to dealing with uncertainty and unpleasantness. To use a basketball analogy, some people prefer to stay out of the fray and pass the ball to another player down court to deliver the bad news. Some who have no one to pass to would rather shoot from a distance than bump elbows under the hoop. Although both options might seem viable, that playbook is flawed.

Some people deal with tough talks by separating themselves from the others involved. Self-preservation-by-emotional-distancing as a defense mechanism prevails among those who know they have to deliver a tough talk—and want to find an escape route.

When you are attached to someone because of blood, friendship, shared hobbies, geographical presence, professional relationships, or work environment, changing anything in the relationship means saying goodbye to it in varying degrees. These kinds of partings involve emotional turmoil. Whether you are bidding adieu to a neighbor who is moving away or an employee whose job is being eliminated, the word goodbye takes a piece of your soul. As a result, it is not uncommon for the boss, neighbor, friend, or relative to distance herself in preparation for a key event. In the following example, this played out around the time my children and their friends were heading off to college.

Dribble & Shoot (cont.)

Tough Talk Problem

Staying connected during times of transition

If you have known anyone who has sent a child off to college, you have probably heard that person say, "He was ready to leave." I remember hearing that comment from my friend, Deb Robinson, when I asked how the mother hen was after Barry, her first-born chick, had flown off to Purdue University. Her phrase, "he's ready," sounded rather noncommittal to me... at the time.

My teenagers were still in high school then and I was already dreading the goodbye that would repeat itself over the coming two years. I really enjoyed all their school activities and the level of energy around our house.

Something happened during the summer between high school graduation and the start of freshman year at college that changed my opinion of Deb's answer. Eagerly anticipating their freedom, the high school graduates seemed to morph into alien beings we did not recognize. The phrase "he's ready to leave" suddenly made all the sense in the world.

At the parents' meeting for Georgetown University that August, my husband and I sat in an auditorium with 500 others listening to the dean of students speak. After welcoming us, he asked, "Have you ever wondered, over the past two or three months, exactly with whom you are living? Who is that stranger walking around in your house?"

As audience members nodded, laughed, and even clapped, the dean explained that it was part of the normal separation process. To protect themselves from the pain of saying goodbye to mom and dad and friends, of moving to the next phase in life, of changing their environments, our young adults coped in the only way they knew how—by separating themselves emotionally and taking on different communication styles and personalities. Thus, the change in behavior indicated they were "ready to leave."

Takeaway

An emotional barrier may mask your pain, but it does not make a goodbye, personal or professional, any easier—just different.

The downside of distancing

It is this same self-preservation-by-distancing mindset that keeps people from visiting a dying friend or relative in the hospital. It also plays a role when you remain civil, yet detached, while in a romantic relationship that has run its course, or when you talk to an employee whose job is on the line. It is uncomfortable to remain emotionally connected. You do not know what to say. So rather than face the situation and maintain the relationship's status quo in terms of everyday conversation, it may seem easier to get angry, act out of character, or stay away. We think doing so makes us or the other person "ready to leave."

When it comes to business relationships, the employee is often not "ready to leave." Thus a sudden lack of communication does nothing for either the deliverer of bad news or its receiver.

Mark Eaton concurs. "There was a time when I didn't talk to my employees much. I didn't want to get too close because I thought there should be a separation between the owner and employee. But I've come full circle. Now I know employees want that relationship."

Maria Pozo-Humphreys states that maintaining an emotional connection is important. "People need to know you care about them and think they're important, even when you're delivering bad news."

All three professional counselors I talked with agree that caring about the employee, although it may compound the angst of a tough talk, is healthy. The human connections cannot be discounted or ignored.

1-shot discussions don't score

A discussion between a boss and an employee is more than just a one-time task; it is a process. All relationships — business and personal — involve communicating regularly. When silence sets in and overtakes the norm, actions get misinterpreted, rumors fly, and stories (often far from reality) get woven in our minds.

"In my experience, the number one killer of business isn't today's economy," says Mark, "but a lack of commitment to communication and teamwork. When you have good communication, you can take on any challenge.

"As a boss, you need to have these important conversations," he continues. "Tough times provide incredible opportunities to get to know key people and build teammates. When you get through tough times together, you become much stronger."

Pitman-Moore's CEO, Bill Mercer, profiled in Chapter 1: *Squeezed & Torn*, consciously chose not to distance himself from his workers. In his numerous trips to visit employees around the world, the emotional benefits and increased productivity that resulted from continuous communication with employees during tough times far outweighed delivering the bad news. By embracing the feelings, attitudes, and concerns of the receivers of these tough talks, Bill comforted everyone around him — even those whose jobs were likely to be eliminated.

How do you see your role as leader?

Pain or relief?

Sometimes what you expect will be interpreted as bad news by the recipient is not. As Ron Culp wrote in the foreword to this book, after one tough talk with an employee the recipient actually hugged him.

In some situations, the energy that has been put into a relationship to make it work — either professional or personal — has not proven to be productive. When the tough talk results in the severing of that relationship, it might be cause for relief.

It comes down to asking, "How is change viewed — as an opportunity to take on a new phase of life or a loss of security?"

Accepting change

Businesses and individuals can miss the omens of resistance.

When trying to accept change, people fall into two camps: those who prefer the status quo and those who look on change as an adventure. I fit into the latter group. As an example, when my husband's employer wanted to transfer him to Kobe, Japan, I was energized thinking about the possibilities of world travel. At the time, Gary had global responsibilities in his job, which took him to various countries four times a year while I stayed home with a baby, a toddler, and two cats. Frankly, I did not find changing diapers or emptying litter boxes as satisfying as I imagined his experiences to be. So when we were asked to move overseas, we readily accepted the assignment. We gave the cats away — but kept the children.

However, telling our parents about the job transfer was a tough talk we had not prepared for. I expected they would be excited for us. What we failed to consider was their reaction to hearing that their grandchildren would be growing up in a foreign land. They were terribly distraught that we would be almost 10,000 miles away. Coming for a quick visit to see us would be impossible. I am sorry to say that I did not position our announcement very well; I just blurted it out on a phone call one evening. I wish I had known the steps to take which could have made the news a little more bearable for them to hear. (These steps are laid out in Chapter 3: *Checks & Balances.*)

Although I can offer no excuse for my lack of sensitivity to their concerns, I am sure that I am not alone in having forgotten that change is not always welcome. It is not just individuals who can make that mistake during a tough talk. Corporations can miss the omens of resistance, too, as the next Real-Impact story shows.

Dribble & Shoot (cont.)

Tough Talk Problem
Getting buy-in for a corporate transfer

Interviewee
Rex Heitz

Organization
Praxair

Beware of sabotage.

The lush, rolling terrain that blends into the foothills of the White Mountains cradles quaint boroughs and mid-sized cities in New Hampshire. Rocky shorelines, maple-lined back roads, and a multitude of recreational opportunities make the state a charming place to visit, and, in many people's eyes, to live.

It was to this picturesque setting that one corporation, Praxair, a supplier of industrial gasses, brought a busload of employees and their families from its Appleton, Wisconsin, subsidiary. In order to fill a hole in its product offerings, Praxair had purchased a New Hampshire-based competitor that had a strong brand and reputation in their industry. Executives had decided to consolidate the two operations, and offered relocation packages to the 20 employees whose jobs were transferable, while providing severance packages to the rest. The company believed their plan, coupled with the inviting New Hampshire location, would make the tough talk about closing its Wisconsin plant more palatable.

The managers believed the engineers, supervisors, and technicians would be charmed by the new area. Who would not be awed by its beautiful rock faces, mountain vistas, and blue skies, or the promise of abundant outdoor activities? The New Hampshire environment, with plentiful hiking, fishing, and hunting opportunities, echoed what the employees knew in Wisconsin. It was a natural fit. Or so the bosses thought.

The reaction from the employees from the Badger State did not sync with the company's expectations. Visiting schools, looking at houses, and exploring the community only solidified the Appleton employees' initial feelings about the move. And they were not positive.

Management had previously estimated it would take six months to make the transfer, thinking that would also give employees in Appleton plenty of time to sell their houses, buy new ones, enroll children in schools, and load up the moving vans. It was a plan that was well communicated and accompanied by a competitive offer, but it was one the employees simply did not buy.

"We totally miscalculated the tremendously strong ties our employees had to their Midwestern community," says Rex Heitz, Praxair's business integration director at the time. "We expected that ten to fifteen key people would immediately see the benefits of the transfer. We didn't think it would be a tough sell. Boy, were we wrong!"

Out of 20 offers only one technician agreed to the move. (Chances are he did not have Green Bay Packers season tickets.)

Praxair, however, would still be moving all production to the New Hampshire plant. In fairness to the employees, the company stood behind its word to keep the Wisconsin facility open for another five months, allowing plenty of time to transfer the technology to the Eastern plant while the employees looked for new employment.

Then, with four months still remaining until the plant shutdown, bitterness reared its ugly head.

"That's when we discovered that the engineering plans sent to New Hampshire to retool the plant weren't quite right," says Rex. "The production results weren't adequate. And the subtle changes made to the specifications resulted in products that couldn't be sold to customers.

"The community's anger over the plant closing poisoned the atmosphere," says Rex. "It was fueling the fires for sabotage."

What did Praxair learn? *"We should have had an alternative plan with a different timeline. If we had to do it again,"* says Rex, *"as soon as we learned that the employees were unwilling to make the move, we should have prioritized the technology transfer of critical applications.*

"Instead of focusing on production concerns, we focused on the human element. And that was not wrong. Even though we knew the employees were not going to move with us, we still wanted to make the shutdown easier for them. We wanted to give them plenty of time to find new work and use the outplacement services."

Rex admits, *"We didn't appreciate how deep seeded their bitterness was."*

The scenic beauty of New Hampshire proved to be in the eyes of the beholder — but only the corporate beholder.

Takeaway

When your tough talk involves a plant closing, you must be prepared for negative emotions and actions. Anticipate repercussions and have alternative plans ready to go.

Dealing with vulnerable employees

What you see is not always what you get.

However positive you *hope* a reaction to a change will be, you cannot assume it will happen that way. It is not just the financial ramifications that fit into the picture, but the psychological ones as well. Identities and egos are often tied to jobs. As a result, being let go, terminated, relocated, or having a salary or work schedule cut can be devastating.

As part of responsible leadership, it becomes your job to think through how employees, especially vulnerable ones, will react to bad news.

Patti Ayars, who has extensive experience in senior HR positions, points out that bosses may only see glimpses of the person's emotional foundation, personality and home life. "There is a lot under the surface. Things have gone on in the past, that you, as manager, do not see. You may *think* you know how they will react. And you may be right. But what you see is not always what you get."

The boss should not practice psychotherapy.

For example, if the laid-off employees are under financial and/or family stress, they may interpret this bad news as a failure, whether or not they had any part in the economic turbulence that caused their employment status to change.

"Even if they don't react negatively," Patti continues, "it does not mean they don't need support from an employee assistance program's counseling services.

"However," she stresses, "it's important for bosses to realize that it is not appropriate for them to practice psychotherapy." In fact, all the therapists and human resource professionals I interviewed stressed this point as well.

Rose Gailey, who has degrees in counseling and organizational psychology, points out, "It's critical to have the support of a professional. You don't know if someone is on the edge psychologically. You don't want to be in a position of assuming a diagnosis. If you see warning signs, you shouldn't be afraid to suggest something else is going on. That's the time to contact human resources or an EAP."

Bad news can trigger mental health issues in vulnerable employees.

Rose adds, "In the general population, mental health issues are far more prevalent than we think. One in five men and one in three women experience bouts of depression. Managers are not equipped to deal with this."

According to a study released by the National Institute of Mental Health, more than half of the adults in the United States suffer from mental or physical symptoms of at least one behavioral-health issue.[1]

Maria Pozo-Humphreys says, "In some cases, dealing with bad news for the emotionally fragile or vulnerable employee may trigger anger or a crisis that can lead to violence, suicide, cutting, alcohol abuse, and other self-destructive behaviors." These are the exceptions rather than the rule. However, it is always good for the employer to be cognizant of the whole picture.

What to watch for

Although it is impossible to list all the warning signs of an employee who may be psychologically vulnerable and thus need professional help coping with bad news, the following questions should be considered as you prepare for your tough talk.[2]

Have there been problems with the employee surrounding
   Absenteeism?
   Habitual lateness?
   Anger?
   Inappropriate speech?
   Missed deadlines?
   Failure to deliver on projects?
   Lack of communication?
How does she handle news that requires a change of
   Behavior?
   Job location (even when in the same area)?
   Tasks or assignments?
Does she deal inappropriately with stress?
Is she quick to withdraw from a situation?
Does your gut tell you there may be reason for concern?

Insights on employment law

Employment attorney Heidi Leithead of Parr Brown Gee & Loveless in Salt Lake City, Utah, advises using an EAP for those who are not violent but may have psychological issues. "Explain to the employees being terminated or furloughed how long they have access to the services and encourage them to call. Have the correct telephone number and other contact information readily available."

Considering the ramifications of the Americans with Disabilities Act passed in 1990, it becomes tricky to involve medical or psychiatric personnel. When discussing employees who have mental health issues, Heidi says, "From the federal perspective, the employer is not required to have a counselor or other medical professional available when conducting a layoff or other termination.

"State laws vary," Heidi adds. "If you reasonably believe some-one is suicidal, you may have some obligation to make sure that person gets assistance before leaving your location. At the end of day, as their employer, you don't want to be thinking, 'I should have stepped in.'"

(Please note that remarks from professionals made here are not intended as legal or medical advice but for general information. Consult with an attorney and/or medical authority in your area if necessary.)

Ensuring security & safety

The security and safety of all involved — the person giving the message, the person receiving it, and those in the office or plant — must be considered ahead of time.

Heidi adds, "When one gives any kind of negative employment news, it's extremely important to have a witness present. Firing someone, laying them off, and giving a negative performance appraisal to a volatile person should never be done in a one-on-one situation."

Before the tough talk takes place, the witness needs to know what will be happening and what his or her role entails. For example, the witness

• May only need to be an extra presence in the room to verify that the information was communicated

• May have to become involved in the conversation if the receiver of the tough talk becomes argumentative and the deliverer is caught in a debate with the recipient

• May need to call in security if the person becomes violent or threatening

• Should be prepared to help the person clean out his or her personal belongings from the work area

Twice in Heidi's 25-year career in employment law she has alerted local police about safety and security concerns. "In one case, we knew the person had access to a gun so the police were in the room during the tough talk. Fortunately, nothing happened. Another time, police were present in the parking lot," she adds. "It's a difficult call, but erring on the side of caution is never wrong."

Tough talks that help business run better

To keep key workers, increase the frequency of tough talks about work performance.

Another type of tough talk that causes anxiety involves performance reviews. Even when they are easy, and the appraisal is a good one, many bosses procrastinate. It is the policy of most, if not all, large companies to evaluate an employee annually; however, that task often goes on the back burner, due to organizational fires that need to be put out. With companies 'downsizing' or 'rightsizing' the workload has increased to the point that many standard policies are ignored in the name of 'expedience.'

Performance reviews are management tools that help a company run better—in good times and tough times. "But the old system of doing annual reviews is broken," human resource consultant Karl Ahlrichs points out. "Successful companies are starting to make changes, primarily by doing them more frequently and with better-defined standards."

The need for quick adjustments in the current environment has accelerated a change in how company performance is evaluated. Just-in-time production, 24-hour access to workers around the globe, and a volatile economy mean that efficiency is a must. No more warm and fuzzy appraisals where most employees are rated "above average." "Tough" and "quick" are the key words.

In addition to changes in the marketplace as a reason for more tough talks, all workers have become used to instant communication. In fact, Generation Y workers do not know a world without technology and instant access. They expect immediate feedback on everything. Thus, work appraisals need to be done more often.

High-performing employees also want to be evaluated frequently, so they can strategically advance on their career paths. And they want the tough standards they apply to their own productivity to be applied to co-workers as well.

In light of how important it is to attract and keep a competitive workforce, putting off the performance talk — tough or easy — is not a wise idea anytime.

Natalie Wilson prepares both herself and her employees for their performance reviews by having them write up the first draft. "That way our dialogue can be structured around our perceptions of the work. I get a glimpse of their thoughts and can plan my comments accordingly." (The evaluation form used at Campus Classics can be found at www.toughtalks.biz.)

Now that you have come to grips with the fact that a tough talk or two is in your immediate future, let's explore the steps to get you through one without such angst. Chapter 3: *Checks & Balances* has a five-step system for you to follow.

Dribble & Shoot (cont.)

• Rumors are detrimental to the team's morale.

• Doubts about the economy turn into fears; fears, into rumors; rumors, into mental paralysis; mental paralysis, into lost productivity.

• Every tough talk has to do with change.

• Whether you are telling someone the job is being eliminated, the marriage is over, or there is no money left in the savings, the emotions and symptoms experienced before the conversation can be as harrowing as the tough talk itself.

• Procrastination is a fairly normal reaction to a difficult talk. It is based on the assumption, sometimes false, that the person who gets the bad news will be devastated.

• Hoping tough times will change adds to procrastination and stress. Move forward quickly once a decision has been made.

• Resentments can build when tough talks are put on hold.

• It is not uncommon for the person giving the tough talk to build an emotional barrier, which does not help anyone.

• Anticipate possible reactions and have Plan B ready to go.

• It is not appropriate to practice psychotherapy unless you are trained and licensed.

• The security and safety of all involved must be considered ahead of time.

• Before the tough talk, witnesses need to know what will be happening and what role they should play.

We know you have a wife who works and a one-year-old daughter who spends her day with the nanny," said the slightly built, college-educated Courtney R. to her boss at a Texas manufacturing company. "Your little girl takes a long nap in the morning and goes to the park down the street at two o'clock… and your nanny doesn't have any protection. So I want you to think about your family when you're considering my performance review.

"Oh, and by the way," she said on her way out the door as an afterthought, but actually a carefully executed comment, "my brother is up in Beaumont," referring to the federal penitentiary. "But he still has friends here."

That is what George S. vividly recalls about a discussion in his office one August day several years ago. A 35-year-old plant manager, George had been preparing for the tough talk he would have with Courtney, a customer service representative. She was on the verge of being terminated for her erratic work performance, not to mention her use of cocaine during office hours. But that day, it turned out, George was on the receiving end of the tough talk.

If that sounds like a scene from a Hollywood movie, the next meeting he had makes it even more surreal. The plant foreman, who walked in as Courtney strolled out, shut the door and announced, "I heard what she said, but you don't have to worry. My 'people' like you. You're a square shooter when it comes to our jobs." Then, trying to reassure George, but actually adding to his anxiety, the foreman stated, "We've got your back. My boys are making sure your family is safe."

Your tough talks hopefully will not involve threats like Courtney's or entail discussions about protection from a gang. And the dialogue might not be as dramatic. But without question, the consequences of disciplinary or termination discussions with employees — as well as standard performance appraisals — impact everyone involved.

On the surface, tough talks at work with the "average" employee may seem less hair-raising than George's experience, but they can still be just as stressful. In fact, standard performance reviews frequently result in a gnashing of teeth and loss of sleep for the boss as well as the employee.

No matter what the situation, when you have to deliver a tough talk, be sure to carefully consider the words you use, the messages you send inadvertently, and the way you deal with the resulting emotions and aftermath.

A 5-step process

The Tough Talks CHECK system is an acronym for:
C=Clarity
H=How to
E=Emotions
C=Comprehension
K=Kickoff

To help leaders understand what to do, I have developed a five-step system for delivering a tough talk called the Tough Talks CHECKSM. It is the result of hundreds of hours of research with professionals from a multitude of business sectors and companies ranging from 25 employees to 46,000. Relying on input from human resource specialists, corporate communication leaders, business owners, managers, psychologists, social workers, and employment attorneys, I have consolidated their wisdom into five elements that must be present for a tough talk to be successful.

If you have previously delivered a tough talk, you will not necessarily remember what worked and what did not the next time around because the human mind is geared to protect us from painful situations. Therefore, it is helpful to have a system for recognizing the dynamics and processes of a successful tough talk and its aftermath. With its easy-to-remember name, the Tough Talks CHECK system also helps you recall how to deliver one.

Although the Tough Talks CHECK system is primarily for the business world, this system also applies to personal tough talks, as you will see in the Real-Impact stories at the end of this chapter. First, let's define the system and then explore each step.

Clarity — being clear about the message, the purpose, and the details

How to — determining the right words and the best delivery

Emotions — allowing for feelings to be processed

Comprehension — making sure the recipient of the tough talk has understood the message

Kickoff — starting the next phase to keep the workforce and yourself moving forward

C=Clarity

For any tough talk to go smoothly, you must have clarity about the issue, the reasoning behind any decision, the process that must take place, and the outcome you would like to see. Think about clarity as the five Ws. When you can answer all five, you will feel more centered mentally as you approach any tough talk you must deliver.

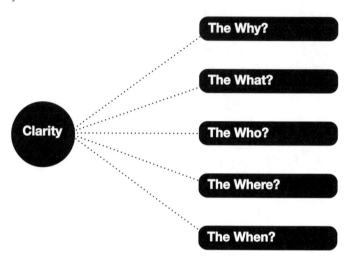

The Why?	Start on your quest for clarity by asking, "Why am I giving a tough talk?" Are you doing it to • Resolve a conflict? • Clear up a misunderstanding? • Critique an employee's work performance? • Improve productivity? • Cut back on salaries or bonuses? • End a work relationship through a layoff or a termination?
The What?	Once you have studied the facts and come to a point of resolution, even though you may not like the decision, you now have to get clarity on the process, the message, and its intent. Asking the following questions helps identify important details: • What has to be addressed? • What does not work in the current situation? • What information and documentation do I have? • What information and documentation is missing?

- What are the specifics of this person's job description that impact this conversation?
- What were the criteria for selecting this person to be terminated or laid off (if applicable)?
- What is the ideal result or outcome?
- What are the next steps to get to that result?
- What if the employee becomes so distraught that he cannot return to the workplace? Are there provisions to allow the person adequate time to regroup?

The Who?

When you know the answers to those questions, you can move into the phase of asking Who?
- Who should be present during this discussion?
- Do I need a witness?
- Is there a legal reason to have another person in the room?
- Are there safety issues which require additional people?
- Is it necessary to have security personnel on call?
- Are HR professionals available to explain the next steps?
- Should an employee assistance program counselor be present or available?

Employment attorney Heidi Leithead suggests having a witness present when firing someone. "Never deliver this kind of tough talk in a one-on-one conversation. Your witness should be able to play another role if necessary. For example, if the conversation becomes argumentative, he or she needs to be prepared to speak up and move the process forward or bring the discussion to an end. And if any threat of physical abuse erupts, this witness must be prepared to step in and call for additional help."

Checks & Balances (cont.)

Who? Me?

Obviously the other Who? in the conversation is *you*. To get comfortable with your tough talk, psychotherapist Maria Pozo-Humphreys suggests asking these important questions: "Who do you want to be? How do you want to see yourself? What kind of person do you want to be in this world, in this job, in this tough situation?"

Consider the options of how you might present yourself:

Factual	Emotive	Caring
Cold	Impersonal	Warm
Dramatic	Restrained	Truthful
Direct	Nurturing	Responsible
Co-dependent	Authoritative	Sad
Funny	Calm	Unreadable
Unflappable	Compassionate	Negative
Positive	Silent	Talkative
Practical	Grave	Reserved
Gentle	Tough	Transparent
Motivating	Sarcastic	Nervous
Realistic	Idealistic	Harsh
Unbending	Detached	Supportive
As a confidant	As an educator	As a parent

The Where?

Being clear about the physical parameters will make your role easier. Visualize where the tough talk will most likely take place. Where is the ideal setting?

- Your office?
- The person's work location?
- A neutral location like a conference room?
- An area where other people are present?
- A quiet, peaceful place?

A neutral location, if available, is often the best option because it eliminates any added psychological barriers surrounding "ownership of territory," a factor not often considered. You will also want to make sure that you have made provisions for an appropriate amount of privacy.

The When?

Determining the timing for your tough talk can add to your clarity. When should this take place?

• Is there an ideal time to deliver bad news?
• Should you get the tough talk over first thing in the morning? Or wait until later in the day?
• Is Monday or Friday better?
• Does a midweek time offer any advantage?

My research shows no consensus on this. To eliminate unknowns that increase your stress, make the decision and schedule a specific time.

Of course, some tough talks happen spontaneously, especially in personal situations, such as disagreements at home. The more adaptable you are to surprises, the smoother life is. Easier said than done!

By spending time contemplating these questions and even writing down the answers, you will move closer to having peacefulness about the situation and minimize any jumbled thoughts or second-guessing.

H=How to

"The test of a truly healthy organizational culture is how you say goodbye to employees," says executive coach Rose Gailey. "It goes back to the values of the company."

For that matter, your personal and corporate values are essential components in how you talk to employees about anything. If you say your employees are your most important assets, treat them as such.

The words you choose for your tough talk and the length of the conversation will vary according to its purpose, which could be to end a personal or professional relationship, to fire employees, to review their performance, or to lay them off.

Let's begin with layoffs, an all too common tough talk in these tough times.

Layoffs

When you meet face to face for this tough talk, it is okay to chat initially, but keep it short. It does not help either party to dance around with niceties. A rule of thumb is to speak no longer than a minute on a subject that does not relate to the reason for the meeting. Idle chatter just adds to the stress for everyone in the room — so the shorter, the better.

"First off, make the global case for why this layoff is happening," suggests Karl Ahlrichs, a human resource consultant. "And then get to the point."

It is critical that the employees realize why you or the company has reached the decision to cut jobs. "Be aware that anything you say can, and will, go public," Heidi Leithead advises. Remember that blogs, tweets, and YouTube postings are pervasive, so chose your words carefully.

For example, you might say something like, "As you may know, our organization is under significant pressure to increase operating profits and productivity. Our market share isn't what it needs to be and that has forced the company to reassess its product line. This changes the need for certain jobs. I'm sorry to say, but as a result, your job is being eliminated."

And then stop talking.

Be aware that the recipient of the tough talk has stopped processing your words at this point. In fact, he may have mentally blocked you out after your first sentence, realizing what was coming next. No doubt he is surprised, even shaken, whether or not he suspected a layoff might take place. Allowing silence at this time honors the individual.

While at Praxair as the business integration director, Rex Heitz was involved in dozens of conversations about restructuring and layoffs. He learned to adjust his style with tough talks over the years. "Early on, I tried to have the initial meeting include all the information the employees would eventually want to know," he says, "such as severance packages and so forth. But I learned that didn't work. They weren't able to process the details. I needed to make that initial meeting brief, then allow for follow-up later with the human resource professionals."

For the small business owner who does not have HR personnel, put the details of the employees' next steps in writing for them. They can refer to it when they are ready. And schedule a follow up meeting to clear up any details.

Terminations

Don't let uncertainties derail your tough talk.

How you handle the tough talk around terminating an employee is certain to test your mettle. Remember, as a manager, you are paid for times like this. It makes the rest of your job look easy by comparison. The reason you are in a supervisory role is that others in the organization believe you have the ability to shepherd people toward productivity. Or maybe it is because you own the company and it automatically falls on your shoulders.

You may question the initial hiring process that put the problematic person in the job in the first place. You may wonder if having a different position or supervisor would have resulted in a satisfactory outcome. You may be baffled about the employee's inability to live up to the expectations of the company, or even dumbfounded by his poor choices.

Do not let these uncertainties derail the tough talk you must deliver. Address these issues beforehand so you have clarity.

As a business owner, your very survival depends on having high-performing employees. Ending a work relationship brings pain, especially in a family business or when you have become close friends with your workers. Firing someone means that trust has been broken and expectations have not been met.

"You're fired!"

Donald Trump might be able to deliver the dictum "You're fired!" with no apparent feelings or repercussions (at least he did on his television show, *The Apprentice*) but as a boss, you do not have that luxury when terminating someone's employment.

If there is one area in which you cannot afford to be without legal counsel, firing is it. In the United States, both federal and state laws cover discrimination, including issues of age, disability, race, color, religion, gender, national origin, family status, family responsibility, sexual orientation, workplace safety, worker's compensation, and whistle-blowing. If you are involved in an international business, terminating an employee becomes even more complex. Get legal advice before taking action.

Security & the walkout waltz

The actual exit of the now-terminated employee is handled in a variety of ways. Some companies do what I call "the walkout waltz." That is when someone is called into a conference room for a long, tough talk; eventually emerges; and then is waltzed out by a security guard to clean out the cubicle or locker as everyone else on the dance floor watches. When the song ends, all the employees are bitter about the cold, cruel nature of your business environment—and maybe you. Unless, of course, the coworker happens to be unproductive, a thorn in the side, a drag on resources, a personal hygiene nightmare, or downright creepy. Then it is hard to stop the applause, or at least stifle the audible sighs of relief.

Certainly there may be legal reasons for an escorted exit, and some situations do call for immediate action. Heidi Leithead suggests that, when an employee is terminated, the person be given the option of returning to pick up personal items after hours or on a weekend with security personnel present for the process. This treats the ex-employee with dignity, which is much appreciated by all in the company.

Performance reviews

Write simple, clear statements of the outcomes you expect from a tough talk.

Many performance reviews are with people who are good workers. Compared with layoffs and firings, performance review discussions may seem easy. But they, too, require a deft touch because you want to choose words that respect the individual. Your purpose, after all, is to improve the productivity of your business or department. (We will discuss how performance reviews can be used to motivate employees in Chapter 4: *Engage & Inspire*.)

When employees have not met expectations and their jobs are on the line, tough talks are necessary so they understand their status within the company. In these cases, you will need to identify the past actions or behaviors that are not consistent with the company's goals and do not meet the standards expected. Then you can spell out what must take place in the future, within a specific time frame. Make the results quantifiable.

State the process this way: "In the next X months, if your job performance has not improved, it will be a sign that this is not the right place for you to work. We will judge that based on these criteria..."

At the end of X months, review the agreement you made with the employee.

More about words used in performance reviews

• Never compare one employee to another during the review. Phrases like "Brenda does a much better job at this task. Why can't you do it the way she does?" deflate the person and may set up an unhealthy rivalry. A better way to get your point across would be to state, "This particular task requires X, Y, and Z for success. Let's discuss X first."

• Do not focus on what you will say to the exclusion of how you will listen. Be prepared for the employee to present new information that is essential for you to consider.

• Present the positive aspects of an employee's performance first. That goes a long way to guiding the employee to improve in other areas. Then be clear about what you want to see changed.

• Keep your next comments neutral by addressing only action steps and skills. For example, rather than saying, "Your desk is messy and you are disorganized," it is better to say, "You would benefit from focusing on your organizational skills. Let's identify a few key steps you can take to move forward in this area."

• The human aspect is key. Put yourself in the employee's shoes. There is never any reason to attack an individual.

• Reinforce your words with written instructions, summaries, or agreements.

You're on stage — so practice

Just "winging it" when it comes to your tough talks, especially ones that will be contentious, is dangerous. Too many key points can be misinterpreted when the words flow out of your mouth or into an e-mail unedited. The end result may not be what you intended.

Your tough talk will go more smoothly if you
• Write down exactly what you plan to say
• Edit the message before you actually deliver it
• Practice it aloud to unveil potential pitfalls
• Learn to listen

Rehearse the tough talk with an advisor or colleague who can point out areas you did not consider. If you are also willing to role-play, the knowledge you gain will be well worth the time you put into it.

If you have delivered many tough talks, rehearsing your words may end up at the bottom of your to-do list. Reconsider. Give it a higher priority. I recently had to deliver a tough talk and, following my own advice, asked a colleague to role-play with me. She was able to point out how easy it was to revert to an old communication paradigm that was not working. With her help, the tough talk that ensued resulted in an outcome that was good for all those involved.

What do your face and body say?

You will find a lot of advice about how body language impacts any communication process. It certainly does in a tough talk, also. Here are a few things to be aware of:

• Show respect by looking the employee in the eye when speaking.

• Sit at the same level with the person to whom you are delivering the tough talk.

• Sit up straight. A slouched posture sends a signal that this discussion is not important to you.

Many more hints are available at www.toughtalks.biz.

E=Emotions

Nothing clears the mind faster than any of these sentences: "We're letting you go." "I want a divorce." "You've got cancer."

When people hear them — no matter what else they were thinking at the time — all communication processing shuts down. Sure, you can keep talking, but the employee, spouse, or patient no longer hears what you are saying. Because the emotional impact is so intense, silence on your part is the only option.

Why people stop hearing your words

Physiologically, when we perceive a threat, our sympathetic nervous system gets activated and a rush of 1,100 neurochemicals is released, according to Deborah Del Vecchio-Scully, who is on staff with Associated Neurologists of Southern Connecticut. The stress response sets off a massive change in our brain chemistry due to a surge of adrenaline, noradrenalin, epinephrine, cortisol, and other chemical compounds that impact us on the cellular level.

Known as a fight-or-flight-or-freeze syndrome, this stress response goes back to caveman days when Homo sapiens had to escape from wild animals. "Today, when we are confronted with an emotional trauma such as news of a major change to our livelihood, our relationships, or our health, there is no place to run or hide or fight. However, the body still thinks it should, so it reacts accordingly," Deborah explains. "This stress response is automatic and immediate."

Once activated, this self-protection mechanism has to run its course. "It is not something we can control by flipping a switch," she adds.

In the fight-or-flight-or-freeze syndrome, this is what happens physiologically:
• Pupils dilate and peripheral vision is restricted.
• Digestion slows down or stops.
• Glucose levels spike, giving rise to a surge of energy.
• The body redirects blood flow to vital areas by constricting and dilating vessels.
• The heart pounds rapidly.
• Breathing becomes short and shallow.

As a result, people can feel faint, have heart palpitations, and may become nauseous.

Time to process

A common mistake made by those who have to deliver bad news is to continue to talk, saying things they should not be saying, and getting off track from the key message. When that happens, the conversation goes downhill fast.

At this point, the deliverer of the tough talk should remain quiet. Any additional discussion points during this time are, at best, useless and can add to the tension in the situation.

It is important for the recipient of the information to begin processing emotions. They may express them in the meeting or contain them until they are out of your presence. But they will come out in some way.

Be clear on your role

When the employee expresses his feelings, it is not your role to talk him through it. This is the time for that person to process the information. Besides, you are not supposed to be trying to make the employee feel better about you. You show the most respect when you act as a professional and stick to the plan.

There is no reason to appear dispassionate or uncaring, even if you feel uncomfortable with emotional displays. You can and should show a sense of empathy.

Maria Pozo-Humphreys says, "It's having a compassionate connection with the employee that helps him absorb the news."

Hidden reactions to tough talks

Psychological counseling is NOT your job.

"Inside a corporation, any of us can be at our worst psychologically and still function," says Rose Gailey. "So it's imperative to be aware that there are at-risk populations in every group. It's critical to have the support of professional counselors, especially during these tough times. You don't know if someone is on the edge. You have to be prepared."

Patti Ayars, in her HR capacity with major corporations, has seen a variety of ways people process the news of a layoff or bad performance review, but categorizes the situation this way: "It's like people go one of two ways; they let their emotions show or they close down. When the latter happens, it's as if a message plays in their heads saying, 'It is not appropriate to show emotions in the workplace.' Those are the people who worry me."

Karl Ahlrichs concurs, saying, "Although they might respond to tough talks quietly, you really do not know what they're thinking. That's a warning flag. You need to be vigilant."

Because few managers and supervisors are licensed therapists, it is important to remember that, even if you have tremendous insights into your workers, you have not been trained to give psychological counseling. Employee assistance programs can provide help. Turn to them whenever appropriate.

When the discussion turns antagonistic

If the conversation becomes antagonistic, bring closure to the meeting as quickly as possible by suggesting a follow-up meeting or providing information about EAP assistance.

Rex Heitz suggests ending the meeting by saying, "The human resource people have more information for you. They will help you understand what types of programs are available for you to move forward." This allows the employee to regain composure.

"It's better for employees to be able to vent their feelings with someone who isn't their supervisor," Rex adds. "HR people are positioned to deal with feelings and provide professional outplacement services and, if called for, help plan for the future."

If you are a small business owner, consider having access to necessary services on a contractual basis.

Security concerns

Patti Ayars experienced situations when the company had anticipated inappropriate reactions during a termination tough talk, so she had security personnel waiting outside the room where the discussion was being held. "Fortunately, we never got a violent reaction and the security people were able to keep their distance. But in this day and age, things happen. You can't take any risks. You must use all the resources you've got."

Larger companies often maintain security personnel on site. If yours is a small company and the employee has a history of violence, Heidi Leithead suggests, "Let local police authorities be aware of the situation.

"Only twice in my 25-year career as an employment attorney have I had to engage police," she adds. "In each of those cases, I was concerned the person might have a gun. Fortunately, security wasn't needed in either case, but it was a precaution that had to be taken."

Comprehension

C=Comprehension

For some bosses, communicating means "I talk. You listen. You grasp everything I say. You act accordingly." Unfortunately, that is not the way it usually works.

The message you have delivered, frankly, is not the point. It is what the other person has understood that matters. Therefore, it is critical to find out whether that person heard you correctly.

This is not about you.

So, to ensure your message has been received, keep these points in mind:

• This tough talk is really about the other person, not you.

• Any feelings of relief that you have delivered the bad news must not get in the way of making sure the information is processed accurately.

• To determine if the person has comprehended your message, you might ask, "Do you have some thoughts about what you just heard?" or "Do you understand what this means?" or "What do you see as your next step?"

• Engage in active listening techniques, such as repeating a few words of the other person's remarks. This often encourages the employee to continue thinking aloud, thus giving you more knowledge about his comprehension.

If you tend to be a consensus builder or people pleaser, be absolutely clear when delivering your message. As Karl Ahlrichs points out, "Bosses who are not comfortable delivering bad news try to dance around the topic and hope the person 'gets' it. Keep in mind that everyone is a selective listener. In tough talks, the subtleties get lost."

That is why you have to make sure the person hears more than the supportive part of the message. Find out if your key point is understood.

Several experts told me stories about employees who did not realize they were being fired. The words used were delivered so cautiously that those involved thought they were on probation. They would say to themselves, "Boy, that was a tough perform-ance review, but I'll get better."

When termination is the reason for the tough talk, you must make it clear that the decision has been made to end their employment. You can still treat them with respect.

Their next steps

In any tough talk at work, make sure you spell out the next steps so the employee has a structure to follow. You should put the details in a formal document, which you both should read. That also visually reinforces your message. Many people do not process information when they hear it alone, but can compre-hend it when they can see it in writing.

• When the tough talk is a performance discussion, you can provide a development plan. Some companies require that the parties involved sign a document acknowledging the discussion.
• When the tough talk involves a layoff, information about unem-ployment benefits or any continuation of company benefits and severance package should be in writing.
• Schedule follow-up meetings so the employee has the chance to get other questions answered or issues clarified.

Your next steps

Although you may be emotionally spent and physically drained at the end of your tough talk, it is not the time to head back to your office and close the door. If you delivered the bad news at any time other than the end of the day, you will probably need a personal break to process your thoughts in order to move forward. But isolating yourself from the workforce for much beyond a short "renewal" time will not serve the company or the morale of the remaining employees well.

Keep in mind that when employees are let go (either from firing or a layoff), the remaining workers have lost their friends. They have spent a good part of their waking hours with each other, in many cases socializing after the job is done. They are mourning the loss of someone who has been more than just a business colleague. As with any loss, they need time to process their feelings.

At this point, your visibility and accessibility is important. Certain situations will call for you to formally address the workforce, such as after a reduction in force. Other circumstances can be mitigated by the "management-by-walking-around" technique, which requires interacting with the remaining employees on a personal basis. Making informal visits to their desks or work stations allows you to listen to their reactions, opinions, and concerns, as well as determine if they comprehend the messages they have heard.

K=Kickoff

The *K* in the CHECK system stands for kickoff—not death knell! It may be easy to consider the tough talk the demise of something—a job, a relationship, a conflict, or whatever is at the core of a difficult conversation—but it can also be thought of as a new start, a new beginning. In fact, the next phase has the potential to be much more rewarding than the status quo, depending on how you decide to measure it.

The kickoff is the beginning of life post-tough talk.

Everyone involved in the tough talk will move forward. That's a given. The time it takes to adjust and adapt to the new situation will vary with individual personalities and the circumstances surrounding the event.

If you think of this step in terms of soccer or football, you can see the possibilities that await every person involved in the tough talk. Even when the first half of a game has gone overwhelmingly in favor of one side, and that team seems to be destined to be the winner of the clash, the kickoff at the start of the second half signals a new phase. Both sides have had time to make adjustments to their game plans and take the field, possibly a bit beaten up, but able to make another go of it.

It is the same with those involved in tough talks. The fifth step, the kickoff, signals the start of a new phase. That does not mean the past is forgotten or the future will not be challenging, but the kickoff does provide a way to think positively about moving forward, even when tough times continue.

As boss, your kickoff has two aspects—very different but equally important:
• Motivating your workforce to pull together and succeed
• Taking care of yourself

In the next two chapters, Chapter 4: *Engage & Inspire* and Chapter 5: *Protect & Defend*, we will go into more detail about these.

The CHECK system in practice

Every tough talk has its own twist. While it is impossible to predict everything that may happen or to detail them all in one book, there are certain common issues that impact many organizations and concern many bosses. More of these issues will be addressed at www.toughtalks.biz.

The following three Real-Impact stories show how the elements of the Tough Talks CHECK system were used in various circumstances. The first two are work-related: dealing with bullies and handling substance abuse issues. In both cases, those involved wished to remain anonymous.

The third Real-Impact story is one that applies to many of us as we care for our aging parents. Although the Tough Talks CHECK system was not even on my mind when my in-laws faced serious health issues, as I was writing this book it became evident that these steps were an important part of what happened.

Tough Talk Problem
Dealing with a bully

Interviewee
Angela F.

Organization
A professional accounting society

When he brought up my leadership style, I could barely breathe.

Angela F. was a people pleaser. Highly respected in her field, she was considered an amiable person who could also speak bluntly when necessary to shepherd projects through obstacles. Even when she was the lead worker on a job, she always made sure that others got their chance to shine.

Angela was asked to chair a committee overseeing a yearlong project for a professional accounting society. On the surface, this should have been a routine undertaking, but the people involved in the project put this confident, Ivy League graduate off her stride.

The project called for innovative thinking that would challenge the society to change its modus operandi. In tough economic times, its membership had dwindled, its resources were scarce, and many of the veteran members pined "for the good old days." The leading proponent for the status quo, Jack, a former officer in the society, was very argumentative as a committee member.

During one conversation Angela had with the colleague-turned-adversary, everything turned ugly. She recalls it this way: "I knew Jack was capable of finding fault with others, but when he turned his venomous comments on me, I literally had an anxiety attack. I couldn't speak. I could barely breathe.

"Out of nowhere, he blamed me for causing unnecessary turmoil by usurping his power," she continues. "We're a volunteer organization. Believe me, there is no glory in this work. But apparently there are politics, and I had no desire to play his kind."

Is someone toxic to your leadership?

When he brought up "what other people thought of her leadership style," Angela was devastated. She was ready to give in and allow the status quo to prevail. Fortunately, she sought the advice of a trusted advisor who knew the personalities of the key players and had experience working with difficult people. Although this advisor was willing to mediate the situation, Angela knew she needed to "buck up" and give a tough talk.

The advisor then role-played a tough talk scenario with her. "It turned out to be a real eye-opener for me," Angela says. "My advisor was able to show me how I could easily be bullied into letting Jack have his way, which I knew was toxic to my leadership role and a step backward for the organization."

So at her advisor's suggestion, she wrote down the following points to prepare for her tough talk:
• This is NOT about me. It is about Jack and his need for power.
• When Jack bullies me, ask this question: "What's in the best interests of the accounting society?" That takes the personalities out of the issue.
• I value his service to the society in the past, but I am ultimately responsible for moving the group forward in the present.
• If he offers to step down from participating, just say "Thank you" and quit talking.

"Knowing what to say and practicing how to address conflict did make the tough talk easier. And learning when to quit talking was golden." Jack later decided to take a sabbatical from active leadership in the society and Angela is back in stride.

Takeaway

Work with an advisor who can help you practice what to say and advise you when to quit talking.

Tough Talk Problem
Confronting substance abuse

Interviewee
Sasha C.

Organization
A Fortune 500 company

Brian T. was a bright, well-groomed, eight-year employee of a software company where he had an excellent work record. He had received raises every year and was promoted to a management position in the procurement area of the firm.

Known as a levelheaded person, Brian suddenly acted out of character when he was chosen to be screened in a random drug test. In fact, he was livid, voicing his opinion that the policy was an invasion of privacy. His concerns were more than philosophical. He was worried that he would fail the test because he had been using cocaine for quite some time.

Brian tried the trick of "watering up" by drinking large amounts of water to dilute his urine, but when the results came out, the trick clearly did not work. He was identified as a user. Sasha C., the company's human resource manager, had to deliver the tough talk.

Sasha was clear about the details of what had to take place because policies and procedures had been set up. That led her to know how to tell Brian what his options were: he could enter an intensive drug rehabilitation program, which the company would pay for, or terminate his employment.

Sasha remembers the emotions involved. Brian argued to be retested, but that was against the company's policy. Then he became extremely angry with her and would not look at her in the eye. He denied that he was user and vehemently insisted there were mistakes with the system, making him a victim. He

Establish guidelines to help ease the tough talks.

even threatened to sue the company. She made sure that he comprehended what steps would be taken because of his actions. He had to face the music: either sign up for the program or sign out of his place of employment.

Approximately a year later, when Sasha and Brian both worked in new areas of the corporation, she heard a knock on her office door. Brian was standing there, asking if he could come in. Although she felt apprehensive recalling how livid he was the last time she saw him, she invited him to sit down.

"He said, 'Thank you for saving my life.' He told me that because of the rehab program, he realized what a horrible path he was on, and if he hadn't been caught, he probably wouldn't be alive.

"That made such an impression on me. I remember the initial discussions when we were setting our policies and procedures. After weighing the issues, we decided that if a random drug screening did turn up a user, the person wouldn't automatically be terminated, but given the option of going through rehab or quitting. There was dissension, but we did come up with a written plan."

As a result of her experience, Sasha now recommends that business owners establish guidelines for substance abuse in the workplace before they need it. "I know Brian was glad we had thought it through."

Takeaway

Establish policies and procedures before they are needed. Then, when tough talks are necessary, there is documentation to fall back on.

Tough Talk Problem
Moving a parent to a nursing home

"I'm glad that man you came with has gone to get some water because I wanted to tell you something," said Artie, an 85-year-old retired banker who was dressed in his usual plaid golf pants and yellow polo shirt.

I wanted to tell you how nicely you have aged.

"What did you want to say?" I asked the man I had known for the past two decades. I leaned forward to catch a whispered comment from the weakened voice of the once-robust person who had swum in the ocean almost daily.

"I wanted to tell you how nicely you have aged. And I didn't want that man to get upset," he said, nodding at "that man," my husband, Gary.

I smiled, though it broke my heart that he could not make the connection that Gary was not only "that man," but also his son.

Even to the end of his life, which was gradually, but not gently, transformed by Alzheimer's, my father-in-law, Adam Heck—known to his friends as Artie—was always positive, complimentary, and concerned for others.

Getting Gary's father to give up his car keys and move into a home for Alzheimer's patients was certainly a tough talk that none of us envisioned. Fortunately, we had the guidance of an expert senior resource counselor to walk us through the steps. Let me explain.

Several years before Artie gave me that unusual compliment, my mother-in-law, Esther, was diagnosed with pancreatic cancer—a horrible disease which usually takes the life of its victim within three months of diagnosis. My in-laws had been living in their Cape Cod home for 30 years. Although Artie was intelligent and conversant in many areas, he did not have a clue how to operate the washing machine or the stove. With Esther's prognosis, Artie would need hands-on training to survive on his own.

Fortunately, Gary's sister, who lived in Boston, was able to come to Cape Cod every weekend to visit her mother and help her father with the laundry and grocery shopping. My husband traveled there every three or four weeks from Indiana. It proved to be a tough time for everyone, not as much physically as it was emotionally.

One weekend when I flew out to visit my mother-in-law, it became evident that Artie needed a different kind of support. Amid the shock of her diagnosis, everyone missed the signs that his issues were more serious than wrinkled clothes and a diet of sandwiches. He was in the early stages of his own cruel disease, which creeps in silently and takes away mental agility, often remaining unobserved for months.

While the family spent time at the hospice center with Esther, I scouted the area for places where Artie could receive care on a temporary basis when the family could not be with him. Fortunately, there was a facility nearby that specialized in patients with dementia.

The senior counselor there explained that Alzheimer's patients are not able to comprehend complicated thoughts. Although washing clothes may be seem easy, it is actually a complex process involving at least eight steps before they are ready to go to the dryer:

- *Sorting clothes*
- *Opening the lid to the machine*
- *Placing the clothes in the tub*
- *Measuring detergent*
- *Pouring it in*
- *Closing the lid*
- *Selecting the cycle and water temperature*
- *Pushing or pulling the dial to start the washing cycle*

Depending on the person's stage of Alzheimer's, just washing the clothes is six or seven steps too many.

The same is true for preparing dinner. Even reheating something in the microwave involves more steps than the laundry, from opening the refrigerator to putting it in the microwave to eating the food. You can imagine the complexity of any directions regarding venting the package, setting the timer and cook level, allowing time to cool, and so on.

The counselor advised us to keep our discussions with Artie about his future living conditions succinct. At most, he would only be able to assimilate three points before he would become confused. She suggested that he be told the following:
• He did not like to cook.
• My husband or his sister could not be there every day.
• He could move into a place that would cook for him.

There was no need to make it more complicated than that because adding our rationale to the discussion would go uncomprehended. And for some Alzheimer's patients, too much information would agitate them.

After our brief discussion, Artie said he wanted to visit the facility. There, the counselor took us all on a tour and answered his questions as simply as possible.

When we went back into the office to discuss the financials, Artie instinctively became the banker again. He asked about monthly fees versus yearly payments. He commented to the counselor, "I bet you'd give me a better price if I signed up for a longer period, say one or two years."

When she agreed, he asked, "Where do I sign? I would like to take advantage of the longer-term rate."

I realize that the majority of similar tough talks with elderly parents do not go as smoothly. But in the process, we did learn how to approach a delicate discussion with clarity. We learned how to say it, were able to allow for emotions, and made sure to simplify the issues so they would be comprehended. These principles allowed us to move the inevitable forward at the appropriate time — in essence, to kick off this new, uncharted phase of life.

I have tremendous respect for professionals who deal with end-of-life issues and I empathize with those who must handle tough talks such as these. I am not suggesting that this is an easy, five-step process. In our case, we were extremely fortunate. I tell you this Real-Impact story to show how it worked for our family. I hope nuggets of it can help you, too.

Takeaway **Clarity about your message, knowing How to say it, taking time for Emotions, and making sure there is Comprehension will allow you to Kick off the next phase. CHECK.**

• Carefully consider the words you use, the messages you send with your body language, and how you will deal with emotions and the aftermath.

• If you have previously delivered a tough talk, it does not mean you will remember what worked and what did not the next time.

• The Tough Talks CHECK system is an acronym for

Clarity—being clear about the message, the purpose, and the details

How to—determining the right words and the best delivery

Emotions—allowing for feelings to be processed

Comprehension—making sure the recipient of the tough talk understands the message

Kickoff—starting the next phase to keep the workforce and yourself moving forward

• Know when to stop talking.

• Get legal counsel when you have to fire someone.

• Rehearse the tough talk with an advisor or colleague.

• Visually reinforce the message you want to deliver.

• The tough talk is about the other person, not you.

• If a conversation becomes antagonistic, it is time to bring closure to the discussion.

• The goal of the five-step CHECK system is to make sure that communication occurs and the message is understood.

| **Chapter 4** | **Engage & Inspire** |

The red tags on the trucks were also symbolic of what was happening to the division.

John McKinney could look out his office window and see thousands of trucks that had come off the production line at the Navistar truck assembly operation. They should have been ready to ship to customers, but they were so far under specifications that they could not be delivered. "Red tagged," they were dubbed in the Navistar corporate lingo — not unlike the color of the ink that was bleeding from the plant's financial statements. John's boss was coming from headquarters to see what was being done to stop the hemorrhaging, and to find out why John was proposing cures that made no sense at all.

"I was willing to risk my job by doing what no one thought would work," says John, who was then the plant manager at the Springfield, Ohio, facility. "So that's what I told my boss."

At the time, the plant was producing approximately 400 trucks per day to fill customer orders. The problem was that the supplies did not sync with the production demand. "Trucks at the end of the line were missing parts, like tires and other essential components," John recalls. Obviously they could not be shipped to customers.

The reason for the failures at the plant had nothing to do with the employees and everything to do with the suppliers. The vendors who produced the components for the trucks had seen the writing on the wall: there would be an oversupply of used trucks on the market soon and they would have to switch their operations to meet the needs of different customers. Thus, they were ramping down their production of parts needed for new trucks.

Everyone in the industry was aware that tough times were coming. At Navistar, production would be cut in half. The truck division would shrink, possibly even disappear. "We could all see the cliff coming up quickly," he says.

When John and his team of supervisors could not come up with any solution to the high number of red tags, he told them, "Our workers probably have the answers." With that in mind, John went to the floor and talked to everyone, department by department, gave them the facts about the situation, and asked their advice—the first time anyone in management had done that.

Having progressed through the management ranks since joining the company right after graduating from nearby Wittenberg University, John knew most, if not all, of the 6,000 employees by name. He had worked the three shifts in every area and had been a part of the community for more than a decade, unlike other corporate managers who came from out of town, stayed for a year or two, then moved on. The workers trusted him.

Ownership of the solution is more important than the solution itself.

"I knew that these employees, many of them third-generation auto workers, wanted to do the best they could," he emphasizes. "When we talked, they were tough on me. I understood their frustration. I could also see the passion in their eyes. There was no way they would let this plant fail even though upper management was extremely skeptical."

Their suggestions were nontraditional, bucked the union, and were counterintuitive to business economics. "They told me, if we have to fix these trucks anyway, let's run them through the assembly line again, use the process we already know well, and hire the labor we need." That did not sit well with management or the United Auto Workers (UAW).

In a union plant, demarcations of labor are strict. If a truck went through the assembly line once and needed to be repaired, only specific classes of workers could be involved. "Pursuing the workers' ideas of redistributing the labor meant going against union rules, and grievances would be filed," John explains. "I respect the union. But these were tough times. We needed to fix the problem by engaging everyone in the plant. I made the decision to do what had to be done and deal with any grievances later."

The UAW got out of the way and let the work go forward. Management got out of the way with their traditional business model. And every metric got dramatically better. "We dug ourselves out the hole in a short time. Within a couple of weeks, we had a totally different operation."

John, who is now president of ICC Bus, a division of Navistar, says, "I learned that ownership of the solution is more important than the solution itself. People want to be a part of a cause that is bigger than themselves. And we gave them that chance at work."

Engagement = motivation

How John McKinney engaged his employees during tough times is very similar to how Bill Mercer, the CEO profiled in Chapter 1: *Squeezed & Torn*, did with his. One acted in his medium-sized American town, the other had a role on the global stage. In each case, they were credible leaders who tapped into the hearts and minds of their employees. That was motivating.

Credible leaders tap into the hearts and minds of their employees.

Moving employees forward in tough times — the K (kickoff) factor in the CHECK system — is the result of a proper balance of inspiring goals and realistic expectations.

Imagine what could be accomplished if the spiral, which illustrated how fears and rumors lead to lost productivity, could be turned upside down. Doubts about the economy could stimulate increased communication; increased communication could turn into the sharing of ideas; shared ideas could turn into plans; plans could turn into actions; and actions could turn into increased productivity.

Increased Productivity

Actions

Plans

Idea Sharing

More Communication

Doubts

The good news is that, unlike the downward spiral where a loss in productivity keeps returning to doubts about the economy, the upward spiral bypasses that and sets up an environment for motivated employees to continue positively sharing ideas, taking action, and growing the bottom line.

The 5 motivating factors you can control

In the current volatile economic times, how much of our motivation comes from our wallets? How much from our need for security and control? How much from our feelings of accomplishment and growth? How much from our own perspective on loyalty? How much is seeing the big picture or tapping into a cause bigger than ourselves?

There are numerous studies that research these questions. The answers all deal with some variation on Abraham Maslow's hierarchy of needs.[1] The following five factors are what employees repeatedly say they want in a job:
- Fairness in compensation
- Fairness in expectations
- Professional development
- Recognition for a job well done
- Care and concern by the employer

As boss, you can make it happen.

Pay, perks & power

Let's deal with the issue of fairness in compensation first. There can be tremendous disillusionment when workers learn of the pay and perks of those with the power in their company. The stories of executives taking home multimillion-dollar bonuses and enjoying luxury vacations, guarded estates, and private jets while the company plunges into bankruptcy or requires a government bailout rankles all — employees and taxpayers.

Even when workers know that the owner of their company, or a leader of their organization, has risen to the top by hard work, education, or financial risk-taking, employees wonder if their own salary and benefits are fair compensation for their responsibilities and workload. When the boss of the company is there because of nepotism, especially if proven to be a poor leader, there is added resentment.

Assuming the compensation and benefit packages for your employees are fair, and are considered so by the workers, they still need to know if the dollars, euros, pounds, pesos, or yen in their paychecks might change during tough times. A large percentage of companies are failing on that front.

According to the research done by Watson Wyatt, only one out of every three companies has communicated to employees how their pay and benefits have been affected by the economic downturn. [2]

But what does it mean to me?

The all-important question, "What does this mean to me?" must be answered. I talked with John Finney, senior communication consultant at Watson Wyatt, about the pitfalls of having employees disengage as a result of not knowing what is happening. "It's all about context, context, context," he insists.

Unless employees understand the whole package, says John, you run the risk that they will leave for greener pastures. You must explain to employees
• How their total compensation package compares to the industry and the marketplace
• What changes are being made and why
• When retirement plans change, what they can do to save in different ways
• The steps needed to take advantage of new incentives
• Whom to contact to get their questions answered

These factors involve compensation issues. Communicating about expectations — the standards required to receive the compensation — is paramount for bosses as well. In tough times, work responsibilities at your place of business have probably changed. The next Real-Impact story illustrates how one company is making sure everyone knows that.

Tough Talk Problem
Understanding performance expectations

Interviewee
Mark Stadler

Organization
American Enterprise Group

On any summer evening when he was not traveling on business, Mark Stadler could be seen by his neighbors planting flowers, transplanting bushes, cutting grass, and handling the upkeep for the home in which he lived with his wife, Jeannine, and their four children. He found it a way to relax after work. Besides, he considered his home his most valuable financial asset and, due to his frequent job transfers, their homes were often on the real estate market. Great curb appeal would help them sell.

His latest house beautification project was always part of discussions at work. Whether it was his droll comments about home ownership or tales of his own escapades as landscaper-in-training (like the time he tried to move a six-foot birch tree by tying it to the bumper of his Buick) Mark's quick wit made him a favorite of coworkers and friends alike. He was great to be around and fun to work with.

"Many days work is no longer fun," he laments, reflecting on the current economic climate. After spending 18 years consulting on business and human resources projects for William M. Mercer Co., Mark answered the call of headhunters and now works in the insurance industry.

"We've just reduced the employee population by 16%," he says of American Enterprise Group, where Mark is chief sales officer. "We're facing unprecedented losses, but see plenty of opportunities for growth. We've let people go who are not necessarily bad performers, but were in areas which are not the core of the business."

Communicating company news to the remaining employees has a significantly different tone than in years past. The executive team, on which Mark sits, asks people to understand key business metrics in more detail than ever before. "We are brutally honest about the reality of the business environment. We have to be."

In other words, tough talks are a way of life at the Des Moines, Iowa, headquarters. The discussions have a frankness about them that could make some nervous about their jobs and the security of the company, Mark admits, "But we need to wake people up. And our employees have told us they have a higher sense of security now because they realize they have control over their own destiny."

The motivating factor is that there is no ambiguity. "No work project is subjective or soft," says Mark. Each employee has a list of specific, measurable objectives that are both short term and long term. In addition, "We've cleared the deck and projects have been streamlined to meet the demands of the marketplace with the number of employees remaining." Each person knows
- *What he or she is responsible for*
- *Who the executive sponsor is*
- *Who else is involved in the project*
- *To whom they are accountable*

For example, there are several critical information technology projects that must be delivered on specific dates, "so it doesn't jeopardize our products," Mark explains. "Our company has had a horrible history of missing deadlines. These dates are not guidelines anymore. They must be met, or more jobs could be lost."

In monthly meetings, the top executives share the financial results with their direct reports, who in turn pass the information along to the next 50 employees who report to them. The flow of communication continues until everyone in the company comprehends where things currently stand.

Their message is clear: The most important thing they can do to protect their jobs is to protect the company's position. "By arming people with the facts," says Mark, "they can understand, adapt, and protect themselves. Because, as I tell my people, your most valuable asset is not your house anymore. It's your job."

Does Mark still work on beautifying his house? "Absolutely. It's a stress reliever. But I haven't tied my car to any birch trees for a while... or begonias, for that matter."

Takeaway **The ability to explain business issues and individual metrics to employees is an essential skill for a leader, especially when a company is in the midst of a turbulent market.**

Your most valuable asset?

Clearing the plate

One of the lessons to be learned from the last Real-Impact story is the importance of right-sizing a job commensurate with any RIF. Workers who survive job cuts are often expected to pick up the slack. It is as if they have one and a half or two jobs, instead of the one they had last year, or last month, or even last week. An essential part of reorganization is being realistic about the number of people remaining to get the work done.

Workers become cynical when their workload doubles but the pay stays the same.

As Mark attests, the diversified insurance company is making an effort to streamline the workload and assess what employees must accomplish. Everyone knows what is left on his or her work plate.

Downsizing in some companies has simply meant doubling the workload on remaining employees. When that happens, the workers become cynical and wonder if those who lost their jobs weren't the lucky ones.

The realistic boss has to make changes to compensate for the fewer number of employees. Without communicating those decisions clearly, as well as sharing how the company will survive with fewer products, services, personnel, and maybe customers, the employees will not buy your explanation of the bigger picture.

Comprehending business economics

Everyone does not have the "math gene."

The American Enterprise case addresses the need for employees to understand the metrics for their individual success, as well as the financial success of the company. When a person's performance is quantifiable, in understandable terms, it is much easier to work towards a common goal.

It is helpful if your employees have a good understanding of how your business works—in good times and bad. Keep in mind that when discussions involve business economics, your workers have various levels of comprehension. Assimilating information about financial measurements may be more difficult for some than you realize. Everyone was not born with "the math gene." Financial literacy is not a given.

You want to motivate your employees when you talk about the company's financial information, not make them feel stupid. Be aware that those who find business economics confusing may be hesitant to share their lack of comprehension with you.

Not all employees understand money

Think about those employees whose skills are at the opposite end of the spectrum from the accountants in your organization. They were the ones who might have come home after school in tears, telling Mom and Dad they did not understand the math problems. And there may be others in your workforce who did not have the advantage of coming home to anyone who was concerned about their education — financial or otherwise.

I recently learned from a person who grew up in the foster care system — and attended many different schools while she was "shuffled around," that no one ever taught her how to balance a checkbook. She admitted having a very difficult time with money-related tasks until a nonprofit agency, The Villages, an Indiana-based organization which supports young adults leaving the child welfare system, provided her with life skills training.

For whatever reasons, your employee population might need a primer on business economics. Training your workers to understand the current economic factors affecting their jobs is an example of professional development — one of the other key benefits employees want from their jobs.

Professional development

Expanding a worker's knowledge base helps your business as well as the employee, especially when she can implement what was learned and share the information with fellow workers.

I am a great believer in the education a person can attain through professional association meetings, workshops, and programs, having seen its impact on my career growth. When these services were endorsed and subsidized at work, it was even more rewarding.

Professional development opportunities are good motivators and loyalty-builders.

Unfortunately, in the "always-on-deadline" world of television news where I spent the early years of my career, there was never any time allotted by my bosses to attend conferences, unless I was reporting on them. Even then, I would have to be in and out of the program, interview the expert and turn it into a news story within two hours. Going into great depth on the subject was not an option. Involvement in my professional association, Women in Communications, where I was an officer, had to be done on my own time. While still valuable, attending meetings after a ten-hour workday or on my only day off was difficult.

When I moved to Eli Lilly and Company I was encouraged by my boss to attend educational conferences. After each conference, not only did I share the knowledge with my peers, I gave summaries to executives at corporate headquarters and, later, workshops to top managers at other locations. That tripled, at least, the value of the conference fees and gave me great exposure to new ideas that benefited the company.

The cheapest retention bonus you'll ever pay.

One of the downsides of the tough times is that employers have cut back on budgets for professional conferences as well as the time away from the office for such activities. Eliminating these valuable programs will prove to be a mistake because of how it affects employee allegiance, especially among high performers. Professional development opportunities are motivators and loyalty-builders. When employees are given those chances, they believe the company cares enough about them to develop their skills. Thus, it addresses two of the factors employees want in a job — professional development and care and concern. Wharton professor Peter Cappelli calls them "the cheapest retention bonus you'll ever pay."

How the educational opportunities are offered — as internal training programs, external meetings, tuition assistance, intracompany cross-training, public seminars, or professional conferences — does not matter. As long as your employees can access them and be able to share their expanded knowledge with peers or supervisors, you will have a win-win situation.

There are many specialists who consult and offer training programs for company-specific purposes, both in person and on-line. Several are listed in the resource section at www.toughtalks.biz.

Recognition

Recognizing employees' efforts should not be a one-time event. It must be part of the culture.

All of us want to be acknowledged for a job well done. Many times a simple thank you will do the trick. But when your own resources — monetary or emotional — are squeezed, stretched, and snapped, expressions of gratitude can fall by the wayside.

Waiting for the annual performance review to share your appreciation is not the answer. By the time the employee's anniversary comes around, chances are you will forget the details of the specific actions that deserve accolades. So celebrate the moment. Do not bottle up your enthusiasm. Stoicism helps no one.

John Schaefer, a human resource consultant and author, warns that bosses who only occasionally show their gratitude do not seem genuine. "Recognition is not an event; it's a process," he notes.[3] Rewarding employees and expressing appreciation for a job well done should be a part of the culture, based on a strategic approach that matches the company's core values and goals.

Gallup management expert Denise McLain says, "If managers aren't able to give employees pay increases or lighten their load, emotional and psychological support is important and may improve productivity."[4]

There are a myriad of ways to acknowledge a job well done. It is important to know how each employee prefers to be recognized. Some like a piece of paper to frame and hang on a wall; others want a private word from the boss.

Engage & Inspire (cont.)

I recently posted a blog request for examples of employee recognition programs or activities that bosses have had success with. All the responses can be found on www.toughtalks.biz. Here are a few of the replies:

Gary Hall of Cattron-Theimeg Inc. wrote:
"With all the layoffs and furloughs that are taking place due to business conditions, the employees are being left to bear the burden. Too many companies these days take employees for granted. I like to send people home unexpectedly with pay, even if it is just a few hours' [compensation]. [Especially on] a nice Friday afternoon. I do this for hourly as well as salaried employees. The unexpected action is the key."

More ideas can be found at www.tough talks.biz

Michael Young of the American Academy added:
"The company I worked for during my college years, Xango, had a great way of recognizing call-center employees who went the extra mile. They converted an empty office into the Snack Shack, which contained a leather couch, a big screen TV, and a microwave, as well as other festive island decorations. Employees could be awarded a trip to the Snack Shack for having a manager overhear them doing something extra on a call.

"The usual 15-minute break was extended to 22 minutes so that the employee could watch an episode of a half-hour show. (The company provided a variety of these on DVD.) In the Snack Shack, they could choose one snack to eat while watching the show. These ranged from popcorn and chips to Hot Pockets®.

"As a manager, I found my employees often striving to go the extra mile so that they could enjoy their next break in style."

Aaron Wandtke of Executive Staffing Solutions commented:
"The need for recognition never disappears. It is just not realized nearly as often [as it should be]. As I see opportunities, I will send handwritten letters to the spouses, significant others, or parents of my staff. My goal is to show my sincere appreciation for the employee [and] also show my appreciation for the [person] who supports the employee and encourages them to do a good job and keep their head up."

John Care of Mastering Technical Sales noted the importance of acknowledging the sacrifices that families have to make.

"One of my better managers, Robb, had to spend a lot of time traveling. He was a good family man. I found out his wife's name and sent her a letter [expressing] how much I valued her husband and his leadership. As a family man myself, I knew the drain that traveling could take on home life. I enclosed a gift certificate for a local movie theater — enough to cover the family plus food for everyone. His wife loved it and sent me a nice letter back. Robb came to work the following Monday with a big smile on his face."

John McKinney, who engaged and inspired the Navistar employees, also focused on families when he wanted to build on the momentum from their turnaround. His group started a Family Fun Day at the plant, complete with games, dunk tanks, music, food, and tours of the site.

"The employees had a different bounce in their steps when they could take their families around and look at their jobs through their kids' eyes. We heard comments like, 'Wow. You get to use these cool tools and build these neat trucks!' Employees could see how impressive their accomplishments were to their families. It was a phenomenal step in changing how people felt about what they were doing."

Care & concern

People don't quit jobs; they quit bosses.

Have you heard this saying? "People don't quit jobs; they quit bosses." The blocks that build the foundation for employee loyalty can only be cemented by those in supervision. Your TLC (tender, loving care) is more important than ever in these tough times.

Employees want to know that the top people in the company care for them and are concerned for their welfare. For those in management who might think that care and concern, other than for safety reasons, does not fall into your bailiwick: it is time to reconsider your position. No person can be productive in an environment where she feels like a robot.

The balancing act

One way to show employees you care is to make the home-work balance a little easier. For most of us, there never seems to be enough time in the day to get the work goals accomplished and still tend to personal matters. Juggling career and home responsibilities takes a toll. The companies that try to make it easier for workers to have well-managed home lives do much for employee morale.

Allowing vendors, such as dry cleaners, on-site availability saves employees much-needed time, fuel, and logistical problems. Additionally, companies with cafeterias that offer prepared dinners to take home at the end of the day have a distinct advantage in keeping productivity high in the last hours of work.

Another way that companies can show support to their employees is by giving them the benefits of employee assistance programs. EAPs are intended to help workers who have personal issues that may result in a loss of productivity at work. Since they are confidential services, the worker can benefit from the privacy that they afford.

Feel the sting & share your bling

No doubt you are feeling the sting of a down economy in all areas of your work and home life. But you still have some of what I call "boss bling" that you may take for granted and your employees may covet. The "boss bling" is the plethora of visible perks, similar to flashy jewelry on the hottest celebrity, that you have earned for the hard work and long hours that come with your job. But in this economy, you must take a look at your trappings from the perspective of your staff members.

It does not matter if your perk is already paid for. What do you have that can go into the community pot for others to share?

Guy Kawasaki, the author of *How to Change the World*, writes that management should be willing to share the pain employees are currently feeling by making sacrifices themselves. Bosses should do something, however symbolic. For example, the noted tech guru suggests, "Give your 30-inch flat panel display to a programmer who could use it to debug faster." You may not realize it, but the value of what you consider a nicety or perk might have better value in another area of the company.[5]

Mike Hanson, a retired pharmaceutical company executive who now serves on the boards of several start-up companies, says fellow board members are tightening their belts, too. For example, they are staying in less expensive hotels on trips, taking public transportation, and having carryout pizza rather than eating in nicer restaurants.

Making the effort to do your part to save money shows concern for your employees' plight in tough times. However, this must be more than a Band-Aid approach. Concern must be genuine if employees are to be motivated by your actions.

Reaching out

Care and concern for the employee is one side of the coin; corporate responsibility, as it relates to the community and the environment, is the other. It is also a favorable feature when employees are assessing the type of organization for which they want to work.

Take, for example, those companies that are actively involved in the United Way or other nonprofit organizations. By supporting those causes with financial donations and volunteer hours, a business not only proves its commitment to being a responsible corporate citizen, it engenders feelings of goodwill in its workers.

A survey of 18- to 26-year-olds by Deloitte & Touche shows that companies who help their employees volunteer their professional skills to nonprofit organizations may have a leg up when it comes to recruiting these Generation Y employees.

• 62% prefer to work for companies that give them opportunities to contribute their talents to nonprofit organizations.
• 82% believe volunteering helps develop leadership and other important workplace skills.[6]

When a company is actively involved in meeting community needs, it also makes inroads with customers and prospective employees.[7]

Care & concern for "green"

Sustainability, the word used to indicate care and concern for the environment, has become a rallying cry of many. Today, being considered "green" is a huge factor in recruiting younger workers. But age is not a predictor of interest in ecology, recycling, renewable energy, biodiversity, and carbon footprints. It is a discussion and cause that cuts across all generations.

As psychotherapist Maria Pozo-Humphreys posed in Chapter 3: *Checks & Balances*, in relation to how you deliver a tough talk, "What do you want to be…in this world?" Her insightful question can also be asked of the company itself as it relates to sustainability. In fact, it is a question that is being asked frequently in employment interviews.

I cannot emphasize enough the importance of communicating with employees. Continuous, honest, understandable, and meaningful communications that are two-way go a long way in motivating your workforce. You have to let employees know what you mean and constantly strive to find out what they are thinking. Without that, no organization or relationship can be sustained. And it definitely will not grow.

The next Real-Impact story shows how one company has kept this in mind and adapted its communications with employees to meet today's concerns.

Tough Talk Problem
Keeping employees informed

Organization
Toyota Motor Sales, U.S.A.

The average employee, five pay grades below the CEO, might not feel comfortable walking up to the company's senior executives in the hallway and asking if what she heard at the water cooler about cutbacks and layoffs is true. That is a discussion very few employees are brave enough to start. But at Toyota Motor Sales, U.S.A., it has become a lot easier to get those nerve-inducing concerns out in the open.

It is Toyota's anything-goes town hall meeting that gives employees a variety of options for having their questions, worries, and anxieties addressed by top leaders.

About 200 employees attend the quarterly meetings, in either the coffeehouse-style cafeteria or conference room, with another 600 seeing it broadcast live across the Torrance, California, campus. Afterwards, the unedited program is sent via satellite to locations across the country.

Six weeks before the quarterly forum, an employee committee comes up with 15 different topics. All employees vote, choosing their top three. Topics may include the fate of the competitors, future product concepts, or dealership issues. And, of course, jobs.

During the one-hour meetings, which are unrehearsed and unpolished, the three topics are conversationally handled, usually without PowerPoint slides, for five minutes, then opened up for a question-and-answer session about the topic. After all three are covered, a no-agenda segment is held. Employees can ask their questions directly, or they can pass them along to Ron Kirkpatrick, the internal communications manager who oversees the town hall meetings.

"Sometimes we lose speed in live presentations because it's unrehearsed and many associates hesitate to walk up to the microphone. They worry about being on TV. So I become their proxy."

Every two years, in an opinion survey, associates are asked, "Is it safe to speak up at Toyota?" Historically, a large percentage said no. "As I told our executives," Ron explains, "'If I were you, that would keep me up at night.' A company that depends on Kaizen must encourage associates to ask questions and voice concerns."

During the town hall meetings, the questions are often hard, sometimes "off the wall," Ron adds. "The executives stare at me when that happens. But I shrug my shoulders, letting them know it is legitimate, and they answer it."

One associate brought up the rumor of relocation to Kentucky, as Nissan had done. Toyota president Jim Lentz chuckled. "I've heard a lot of rumors," he told the audience, "but not that one."

He assured them that they had so much investment in the Torrance area, "There is no way we would uproot the company and go elsewhere. We couldn't possibly save enough money by moving locations."

Along with the town hall meetings, an intranet forum allows associates to post questions, either to a specific executive or the group in general. Answers are usually handled within 48 hours.

What are the lessons from these employee communications that Toyota leaders can pass on to owners and managers in other organizations?

"It is really important to get out in front of employees and talk about any issue bugging them. The more often you can do this, the fewer rumors there will be. Simultaneously, those managers who spend time learning about employees' hopes and fears can be much more effective," observes Ron.

Takeaway **Open dialogue allows bosses to dispel rumors and assure employees about the future.**

Traits of exemplary leaders

We have looked at how employees are motivated from the perspective of compensation, fair expectations, professional development opportunities, recognition, and feeling cared about by
their management—all factors that engage your workforce.
Engage is the one of the words in this chapter's title. *Inspire* is
the other. Let's take a closer look at that.

Most bosses would probably not consider themselves inspirational. In fact, the word itself makes them uncomfortable. After
all, they think, the people who are inspirational are the ones
written about in history books: Martin Luther King, Mother
Teresa, Winston Churchill, and Mahatma Gandhi, for example.
Well, guess what? It is time to come to grips with the fact that
leaders of companies are expected to be inspirational as well.
Especially in tough times.

Leadership traits have long been an area of study for Barry
Posner, dean of the Leavey School of Business at Santa Clara
University, and Jim Kouzes, executive professor. They have
done original research for more than 25 years and have
collected data from more than 3 million people. Their early
findings have been reinforced over the years. They emphasize
that if bosses are to be leaders, they have to be highly credible,
forward-thinking, and team-oriented—and inspiring. Jim Kouzes
writes in his blog:

"People expect their leaders to be enthusiastic, energetic, and
positive about the future. [It signals] the leader's personal commitment to pursuing the dream. If a leader displays no passion
for a cause, why should anyone else?

"Being upbeat, positive, and optimistic about the future…is
crucial at any time, but in times of great uncertainty, leading with
positive emotions is essential to moving people upward and
forward. Leaders must breathe exuberance and life into our
hopes and dreams and enable us to see the exciting possibilities
that the future holds."[8]

Leading by example, without giving instructions, is a job half-done.

More than just walking your talk

When it comes to motivating your employees, high credibility is an essential attribute. The well-known saying "Actions speak louder than words" is important, to be sure. But as a boss in today's YouTube world, you must go beyond.

You must walk the talk, yes, but also talk the walk. Without good communications being foremost on your mind as boss, you run a very strong chance of having your actions misinterpreted or missed altogether. Leading by example, without instructions or inspiration, is a job half-done.

Your employees want to be inspired by your encouraging words.

Know your speaking strengths

Are you better with a scripted speech in front of a large group or in a question-and-answer session with a small group? Some people think that the communication skills required are the same. They are not.

As a communications advisor and executive speech coach, I am keenly aware of the strengths and areas for improvement each person brings to the table. Your communication strength might be speaking one-on-one or in small group settings. You may excel with two-way exchanges, keeping your answers short and allowing for give-and-take among the group. Or you may shine when you address a large audience, using the appropriate blend of statistical information and cogent stories. Your audiences may put away their text messaging devices and cell phones and hang on your every word, remembering it months later.

The best communicators can do both. Have someone — preferably not a person who reports to you or lives with you — give you honest feedback. It is essential to know "the good, the bad, and the ugly," especially when it comes to delivering tough talks.

Share your vision

As John McKinney noted at the beginning of this chapter, "People want to be a part of a cause that's bigger than they are." He engaged the Navistar employees by giving them the chance to take control. He inspired them to succeed at work during a very tough time, despite historic management-union tensions, supply issues, and negative market forecasts.

Maril MacDonald, human resource strategist and CEO of Gagen MacDonald, sums it up this way: "People will work for a paycheck, but they will fight for a cause. What many companies forget is that they tend to make the cause so small that no one wants to fight for it."

Economic concerns are leading employers to focus on what it takes to succeed by working harder and saving costs. But these tough times also provide opportunities to talk about where your organization will be in the future. Most important to the discussion is why the destination you are striving toward is worth the fight.

What is your destination? Do your employees know what it is? Are they willing to fight for it alongside you?

Communication: The central theme

By now you have realized that engaging and inspiring employees involves communication. It is at the center of everything.

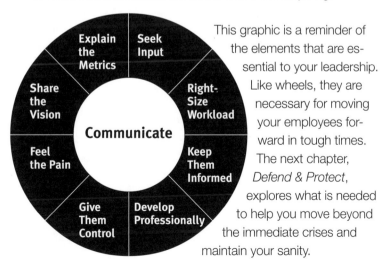

This graphic is a reminder of the elements that are essential to your leadership. Like wheels, they are necessary for moving your employees forward in tough times. The next chapter, *Defend & Protect*, explores what is needed to help you move beyond the immediate crises and maintain your sanity.

Engage & Inspire (cont.)

• People want to be part of a cause bigger than themselves. If they can find that in the workplace, they will be more engaged in the company's mission.

• Moving employees forward in tough times is the result of a proper balance of realistic expectations and inspiring goals.

• Credible leaders tap into the hearts and minds of their employees.

• The five motivating factors you can control are:

1. Fairness in compensation

2. Fairness in expectations

3. Professional development

4. Recognition for a job well done

5. Showing care and concern

• Two out of every three companies have not communicated to employees how their pay and benefits have been affected by the economic downturn.

• The realistic boss has to make cuts in the workload commensurate with the personnel remaining.

• Professional development opportunities are motivators and loyalty-builders.

• You must walk the talk — but also talk the walk.

• Continuous, honest, understandable, and meaningful communications that are two-way are the most essential element for survival in tough times.

Chapter 5   Protect & Defend

The North Vietnamese Army was making significant strides in 1967 in its seemingly endless war with its neighbors to the south. Three battalions of United States Marines were positioned near DaNang to block the North's advances. They and other units from the same division had been in that particular region for nearly two years. Although they all had seen action throughout their 20-month deployment, their current duty status was a "keep and maintain" mission.

Stray dogs roamed the area, looking for food. Or used to. These Marines, finally able to stay in one place for a while and wanting something to feel a little more like home, began taking the dogs into their tents behind the wire. They would bring back leftover food from their meals in the mess to feed the dogs. They eventually bonded -- which was a win-win situation for all. The Marines got pet companionship and the dogs got food and shelter.

One day orders came down from Division Command sending the Marines north to the Demilitarized Zone. The orders did not include the dogs, so their "jobs" as pets had come to an end. There was no Humane Society of South Vietnam to find them new homes.

These canines, left behind and on their own, would become dangerous to the Vietnamese society because the feral dogs would quickly form into packs. If the dogs journeyed north with their providers into combat, they would give away the Marines' position and thus pose a liability — a deadly one at that.

The decision was made in a matter of minutes. The troops were headed north that afternoon, and the dogs had to be terminated. The duty of "letting the dogs go" fell to a corpsman who knew what had to be done and volunteered so that the other Marines would not have to face the grim task. He was told by his commander to shoot them. If nothing were done, the rural population around DaNang would be at risk and the lives of the brave men heading into hostile territory would be in even more peril. A Navy chaplain assigned to the unit remembers it this way:

"These big tough Marines, who had seen the horrors of war, teared up like kids when they had to turn their dogs in. I still remember hearing those gunshots. We all knew what was happening.

"The troops did not seek solace from me, however. It was the corpsman who suffered most and asked for my counsel. He understood his mission to eliminate the animals in order to save lives. But he was trying to deal with the fact that every person in the battalion looked at him in a different way. He was the guy who killed their dogs. They didn't hate him; nor were they angry. But he said he would get a look from them that drove him crazy."

The feelings that the corpsman had are echoed throughout the business world. The bearer of bad news or the person assigned to put the execution of orders into effect suffers a different sort of consequences. It is called survivor's guilt.

Surviving survivor's guilt

Survivor's guilt is triggered by lack of closure and, possibly, feelings of inadequacy. It impacts the bearer of bad news, the work environment, and family life. Financial ramifications aside, how do you as a manager get through this guilt without having the stress destroy you and, potentially, your family?

The answer to that question goes back to the elements of the CHECK system, specifically to the actions surrounding your clarity about delivering the bad news and how you handle your emotions. With that, it becomes the kickoff to your self-care plan.

Clarity—	**How to—**	**Emotions—**	**Comprehension—**	**Kickoff—**
being clear about the message, the purpose, and the details	determining the right words and the best delivery	allowing for feelings to be processed	making sure the recipient of the tough talk has understood the message	starting the next phase to keep the workforce and yourself moving forward

Completing the process itself is complicated by the volatile, rapidly changing business environment. Down time is a thing of the past and our work lives are filled to the max. If you do not carve out the time to go through the entire CHECK process for yourself, survivor's guilt will not be put at bay. It will be detrimental to you and everyone surrounding you.

What everyone is thinking

You might be thinking that you could be next in line for the bad news yourself. As author Guy Kawasaki writes, "After the layoff, this is what the remaining employees will be wondering about:
1. Why did I survive the cut and my colleagues didn't?
2. Will I survive the next round if there are more cuts?
3. Will the company survive at all?"[1]

If you are the owner of the business, the third question has always been on your mind—even longer than the current economic downturn. In these tough times, finding the antidote to market woes takes on even more urgency.

With those constant concerns, your own health—mental and physical—is at risk. No wonder one boss summed it up this way: "I'm exhausted at the end of the day. I never imagined it would be so hard at this stage in my career. This is totally different from what I had planned."

Adding to the stress of the economic ramifications is the fact that we are a society that does not turn itself off. We have our cell phones with us constantly, check our e-mails after work and on vacation, and want instant access to what is happening in the news—even when the very nature of news reporting centers around change, most of it unsettling.

We can become overwhelmed by this data assault, or we can take the actions necessary to protect ourselves.

Your kickoff — or kick-start

"Those who say these stresses don't bother them are in denial," says counselor Deborah Del Vecchio-Scully. "Some people do get conditioned, or even tough," she admits, "but I think they'll end up in world of trouble one day."

Are you doing what is necessary? This is the time to kick off — or maybe kick-start — a self-care plan.

You are what you think

Before we get to some of the steps you can take, we need to look at how your thinking affects your survival.

Rose Gailey, executive coach, says that people experiencing survivor's guilt are actually unaware of how their own thoughts are creating their reality. "Without awareness of the impact our mindset has on any experience, we tend to see events as a simple cause-and-effect matter. It's so much more than that." In other words, we are what we think.

A hypothetical scenario

Carve out the time to ensure the front and back ends of a tough talk are adequately talked through.

Let's play this out. Say, for example, you are a manager who has to lay off five people who work in your area. You know that tough times are taking a toll on business, but you are not privy to what decisions were made by your supervisors in choosing whose jobs would be eliminated, nor were you given a solid understanding of the strategies to keep the company solvent. Due to time constraints, you have a rather cursory meeting with the human resource people, limited to a quick review of legal issues. Then you call the employees into your office to deliver the bad news.

You feel horrible about what is happening and think about the effect it wil have on the employees' personal lives. You may even wonder how they will find other employment. "Your experience of the event is totally based on how you perceive it," says Rose.

Your employees, obviously, think about the situation from a different perspective. But let's take the scenario down a route that is less predictable — that they are not devastated by the news.

Assume they are somewhat pleased, because they anticipated the layoffs, have their own back-up plans, and are content with the severance packages.

Does that mean you will not suffer survivor's guilt? Not necessarily. Since you were not adequately prepared for the tough talk from the outset, you personally are still back on step one and have not yet found clarity. You also might have struggled with how to deliver the news and you have difficulty processing your own emotions. As a result, you may readily suffer from survivor's guilt.

It is extremely important that you have clarity ahead of time about the circumstances that resulted in the layoffs. You must comprehend
• What the business challenges are
• What options were considered
• Why the strategy is being implemented
• Where the company is headed

Better still, if you have been given the opportunity to talk through the issues—and possibly debate the decisions with other managers or your boss—you will become clearer about the tough talk itself and your role in the bigger picture.

"That doesn't mean you'll like the decision, or even agree with it," warns Rose, "but you'll be much better equipped to take part in the process and not feel guilty about your role. The pre-work is critical to the tough talk and to your survival."

Equipping yourself to survive

Just as the pre-work was necessary to ensure clarity before delivering the tough talk, there must be follow-up. Rose suggests, "There should be a session or a phone call, some touch point that explores the event at a thinking level, not a cursory review of whether you took care of the legal requirements. The 'bearers of bad news' should be given the opportunity to debrief and process, as well as understand their own roles in the events. They should be coached and given guidance about how their perceptions will impact their own resolution of the tough talk. This equips them to be survivors who don't harbor guilt."

How stress experts process their own stress

When your emotional gas tank is empty, where do you turn to fill it up?

When you feel like you must exert more mental and emotional energy at work than you can muster up, what you do for yourself is a key factor in whether your company, career, and possibly your family will make it through tough times.

I asked Maria Pozo-Humphreys what "stress experts," counselors and psychotherapists like her, did when they were overwhelmed.

"Let me tell you about a day I had a couple of weeks ago," she said. Normally an optimistic and energetic person, Maria felt emotionally depleted after a particularly rough morning. It just so happened that the patients she counseled had stories very close to her own.

Her first patient had just lost his brother and needed her guidance to help him through the pain. Maria knew that pain intimately. A few years prior, her own brother, who lived in the Dominican Republic where he ran the family's business, had been accidentally electrocuted as a result of the country's notoriously substandard power system. Maria still felt the loss sharply. Her other patients that morning were also in crisis situations and she was emotionally drained by the time the lunch hour rolled around.

Talking to someone honestly and openly is an essential part of protecting and defending yourself.

"What do we therapists do to keep ourselves moving forward on days like that? We go to someone else to help us process and help us talk it through," Maria said. "Even if it's for a brief time with a colleague, I need to get support from someone who understands when my emotional gas tank suddenly registers empty."

"I maintain the confidentiality of my patients, but I do need to be able to sit with my colleague and know that she can relate to my stress, pain, and exhaustion."

"I was wiped out. I went to her office and said, 'I need you for five minutes.' As I sat down, she walked over to me from behind her desk, positioned herself directly in front of me, and gave me her undivided attention. I talked and she listened."

"The people who have to deliver bad news are in a similar situation," Maria commented. "These bosses need to take care of themselves, which means they need someone to share their experiences with. Someone to help them process their feelings."

Don't internalize, ignore, or numb your feelings.

"This is often harder for men than women. But no matter what gender, those bosses who internalize their stress or anxiety can end up in worse shape than those who have lost their jobs. It becomes very easy to drink too much, eat too much, do anything in excess, hoping to numb the pain. These excesses can lead to heart attacks, ulcers, angry outbursts, and a whole host of other problems."

"Internalizing, ignoring, or numbing your feelings doesn't work, because they just go underground and come up at later, perhaps inappropriate, times."

It is important to have the opportunity to work through your feelings about surviving the job cuts or salary caps or increasing work responsibilities.

Key mental health tips for bosses[1]
• Find a colleague to debrief with. If you do not have anyone at work, someone from your professional association may be ideal.
• Talk to your spouse or significant other about your feelings and concerns.
• Keep your social network strong.
• If you do not have anyone to talk to, there are licensed mental health professionals in every town who are trained to deal with such issues.
• Take time for fun.
• Set aside a specific time to contemplate, meditate, or pray.
• Reduce your time in front of the computer screen and television.
• Volunteer to help on a charitable cause.
• Get seven or eight hours of sleep each night.
• Exercise.
• Determine what you can and cannot control.
• Get 15+ minutes of sunshine each day.
• Learn how to control negative emotions.
• Spend time with positive people.

Mindless distractions

It is easy to think that distractions are an effortless way to relax. "People frequently use the internet or addictive computer games, for example, to avoid stress," adds Deborah Del Vecchio-Scully. "They think these distractions clear their minds. They really don't. Even if their minds are occupied by a TV show, for example, the body still activates the stress response."

In other words, watching a "mindless" TV show or movie is just that: mindless. It does nothing to release good neurochemicals, like endorphins, and therefore does nothing to relieve the stress.

The important question to ask is: Are you doing the right things for your heart, your mind, and your soul?

Your marketability

Having your own "Plan B" during these tough times will help you with stress relief. Knowing your skill set, taking steps in professional development, and being able to articulate your value will go a long way in helping you sleep at night.

Tough talks have their upside

Despite the fact that you probably do not like delivering tough talks, it is a core skill in today's economy. It adds to your marketability. Being able to handle difficult subjects and conversations can differentiate you and keep you moving your career forward.

Karl Ahrlichs, human resource consultant, calls this "a core skill that will keep you on board longer than someone who doesn't have this ability. Not only will your division perform better, the organization will recognize managers who have this skill."

CEOs in all sectors are concerned with performance management. The ability to keep, motivate, and engage good employees is essential. If you have a good track record in this area, you stand a much better chance of surviving in these tough times.

The boss who is able to guide employees toward increased productivity will have another arrow in his quiver when it comes to leadership skills.

Define, articulate, and practice talking about your professional value.

Do you know what makes you a valued employee? Define it and articulate it. Put it in writing and practice the self-talk that goes with it. Tooting your own horn, or having the ability to brag about yourself, is often very difficult. Learn how to do it now when your job is not on the line. (Go to www.toughtalks.biz for more tips on improving your marketability.)

Even if you do not expect to be looking for a job, it never hurts to get your résumé in order. A professional service can help you find the right words and approach. It is worth the investment to have this important part of "Plan B" in your back pocket.

The ball is in your court. What are you doing to increase your marketability?

Tough Talk Problem
Defining your own strengths

Interviewee
Mark Eaton

Organization
UCLA and the Utah Jazz

You would think that a 7'4" basketball player would be a tremendous asset to any team. That was not always the case with Mark Eaton. He did not know what his expertise was beyond being tall. When Mark transitioned from a junior college to UCLA, he spent most of his time on the bench. He knew he could contribute, but he did not know what differentiated him from the other players.

On summer afternoons, it was not uncommon for the "old men" to come out for pickup games. The "old men" were UCLA graduates who had retired from their own professional careers and still enjoyed the camaraderie and competitiveness of the game that made them famous. The current students often played with them.

One day Mark was huffing and puffing his way up and down the court, trying to keep up with the shorter (barely) and much quicker players. Just about the time he would get to one end of the court, a basket or a turnover would be made and the players would be on their way back down to the other end of the court. Big Mark would start back in that direction. The "rabbits" would pass him by and get to the basket before he did, shoot or turn over the ball, and start heading back. So Big Mark was not spending as much time with the ball as he was running back and forth trying to keep up.

One day while on the sidelines catching his breath, Mark felt a huge hand on his shoulder. He looked back to see the legendary Wilt Chamberlain standing there, saying to him, "Man, you are never going to catch up with them. But that's not your job. Your strength is not making baskets. It's preventing them. Play defense. Guard the paint."

That moment everything changed.

With that great insight, Mark found his niche and capitalized on it. He spent his time at the opponent's basket, wreaking havoc with their game plan, adding chaos to the mix and keeping the ball out of the basket. He would retrieve the ball and throw it to his own guard, whose niche was to take it downcourt and score.

"That moment everything changed. I went from a guy just playing basketball to defining my own niche — defining one thing I could be great at."

"Even though I knew what I was supposed to do, the coach at UCLA kept me sitting on bench most of the time. As a result, I had to market myself to pros because no one from UCLA really knew my true value — except Wilt."

Mark went on to play for the Utah Jazz for 12 years, be named Defensive Player of the Year for the National Basketball Association twice, and break the NBA record for most blocked shots in a single season.

Mark found his niche, marketed it, and had a very successful career.

Takeaway

Find your niche, hone your skills, and learn how to demonstrate and articulate your value.

Protect & Defend (cont.)

Lifeline relationships

Having a relationship with someone at work from whom you can get advice on your career is priceless. Unfortunately, that might be hard to find during tough times. As companies cut down on workers, there is less time for experienced workers to take younger employees on as mentees.

The problem of finding competent advisors is compounded for business owners who have few, if any, employees. The "solopreneur" is left to make all the decisions. It can be lonesome, even with the digital connections that abound. For business owners who employ only a dozen or so employees, it is not unusual to be peerless.

Are the people surrounding you toxic or inspirational?

I have been lucky to have wonderful professional colleagues in my life off whom I can bounce ideas and brainstorm. Currently I meet once a week with three other businesswomen, all in different professions, who live within a five-mile radius. Keith Ferrazzi, author of *Never Eat Alone* and *Who's Got Your Back?* would call them my lifelines. We meet for 90 minutes at the beginning of each Wednesday and focus on business issues. We share ideas from thought leaders that might aid in growing our companies.

The group started because I wanted to surround myself with optimistic people. This was during the stressful times when my son was deployed to Iraq and Afghanistan and I knew having positive people around me would be good for my psyche. I knew all the other women. They were caring, smart, kind, focused, fun, and funny. In the time we have been meeting on a regular basis, we have developed a deep bond that has transcended business and led us to work on personal development as well as professional growth.

Mastermind groups

Another type of informal mentoring can be found with groups that have been termed "masterminds." In my case, I am a part of one that consists of six business owners located around the country. We met through our professional association, the National Speakers Association. We all make presentations to a variety of audiences, but we each have our own speciality. We meet each month virtually via Skype™ connections on the Internet, and get together in person once or twice a year.

Both groups work well because of four essentials:
• We maintain confidentiality.
• We are generous with our time and talents in helping each other.
• We are able to be candid with each other, while being caring and cognizant of one another's feelings.
• We hold each other accountable. We each set our individual goals, but report our success or failure to the group.

Mini-vacations & major getaways

Patti Ayars, transformational change agent, likes to say that energy is her most valuable asset. "As a leader, if your energy is depleted it is hard to bring energy to other people." Without that, business will stop moving forward.

It is extremely difficult to keep energy levels up for at least 16 hours each day, seven days a week, 52 weeks a year, without breaks. Relaxation experts suggest taking mini-breaks and mid-level breaks along with your usual vacation time. Here are some ideas:

Mini-breaks
• When you are plunged into a stressful situation, take a couple of deep breaths.
• Get away from your desk or workplace every 90 minutes. A change of scenery for ten to 15 minutes is refreshing.
• Take an instant respite by closing your eyes and imagining a different setting. Pat McHenry Sullivan, author of *Work with Meaning, Work with Joy*, offers advice on how to do this at her web site. Her two-minute retreat is reprinted in an appendix of this book.

Mid-level breaks
Several bosses I know changed their getaway times to include more breaks from the office, but made them of shorter duration. They go on three- and four-day vacations, rather than spending multiple weeks away from the office. This allows them to focus on themselves, their families, and their friends, while leaving work behind. It is the mental break as much as the physical break that helps.

Figuring out your puzzle pieces

Finding the time to get everything accomplished during the week is often like figuring out a giant puzzle. Which pieces go in the center? Which should go off to the side for a while, until it is more advantageous or efficient to include them? Which will work together seamlessly? Which seem impossible to fit?

You have absorbed a lot to think about during these tough times. What does the puzzle of your career and life look like now? What will it look like a month from now? A year from now? Even at the end of your career?

Creating your own job & life parameters

Cali Williams Yost, author, president of Work+Life Fit, and Fast Company blogger, has been doing research in this area for 15 years. These tough times have brought many changes. "We're seeing individuals do more to manage their own careers. If you think of it as a professional highway, sometimes you're in the fast lane; sometimes, in the slow lane. Sometimes you might stop at the side of road, voluntarily or involuntarily. There are all sorts of resets on the work+life highway."

Cali shared examples of her recent findings:
• Groups of people have gone to their managers and said they will each work one less day a week if it will save jobs.
• Those who are in the midst of personal transitions, taking care of a new baby or elderly parents, for example, have presented plans to their employers to work from home one day a week or share their jobs with others in similar positions.
• People have taken severance packages and become consultants who can work on a project-by-project basis.
• Others have come out of retirement to shore up their 401(k)s and do seasonal work, such as being inspectors at manufacturing companies during busy times of the year.

Beyond career planning

The big picture is about how can you protect yourself in all areas. Cali breaks it down into three essential elements:

1. *Physical.* You cannot do everything harder and faster and think it makes your job safer. It just makes you tired and unhealthy. Exhaustion does not work. You need to have regular exercise, have a consistent sleep schedule, and eat right.

2. *Community ties.* Developing and sustaining community ties multiplies your support system. Too many people have their primary ties through work. In this current economic climate you must have a strong group of family and friends, so when you are on the receiving end of a tough talk, you might only lose your source of income, not your source of emotional support as well.

3. *Spiritual grounding.* This dimension does not have to be tied to traditional, organized religions or places of worship, although those do provide an essential connection for many people around the world. Setting aside time for quiet, meditation, or prayer on a consistent basis can give you a tremendous sense of peace, as well as inspiration.

"I worry that people who are not making sure these things are a part of their lives will not survive tough times. It sounds really dramatic, but I don't want to underestimate how critical it is that we learn skills to take care of ourselves," says Cali.

Your tough talk

The reality is that we have to take the lead on our own behalf.

Preparing for a tough talk, delivering the bad news, motivating a workforce, and keeping your own mental and physical health in order is not easy. It requires conscious effort. That may require a radical change in your thoughts and actions. But the massive upheaval of the economic and sociological environments in which we do business today means it is time to learn a new game.

You would not have read this far if you were satisfied with the status quo. So it is time to change. You have been given a system to handle the inevitable difficult discussions that come your way and advice to make the aftermath of them fruitful. Now put the Tough Talks CHECK system to work. Let me know how you do. I look forward to hearing from you.

Jean Palmer Heck

Protect & Defend (cont.)

• Survivor's guilt can be triggered by lack of closure and feelings of inadequacy about how you handled the tough talk. It affects the bearer of bad news, the work environment, and personal life.

• Tough times and the tough talks about them are not a simple cause-and-effect matter. Your thinking plays a significant role.

• The work before and after the tough talk is critical to your survival, but often neglected.

• After the tough talk, you must debrief and process, as well as understand your own role in the events, to prevent survivor's guilt.

• Watching a "mindless" TV show or movie does not help relieve stress; it only postpones it.

• Internalizing, ignoring, or numbing your feelings doesn't work either. They just go underground and come up at later, potentially inappropriate, times.

• Have your own "Plan B."

• Know what makes you a valued employee and be able to articulate it. Find your niche, hone your skills, and learn how to demonstrate your value.

• The upside of delivering tough talks: It is a core skill that can differentiate you, which adds to your marketability.

• Surround yourself with optimistic people and convene a "mastermind" group.

For any leader to make an impact on the workforce, the community, or the world, it takes the ability to communicate well. Easier said than done. Technological changes have given us the means to communicate quickly on many different levels to many different audiences. While some of those communications need to be detailed and complex, others need to be short and to the point. It is the latter that stymies most people.

The ability to condense information into succinct answers that get the message across so it can be repeated and remembered requires a special skill set. Today's audiences expect their information in sound bites, bullet points, tweets, and tag lines. You cannot lead them if you cannot speak their language.

Having been a corporate spokesperson, I know how hard it is to package complex information into short, understandable quotes. Few leaders do it well — with the proper blend of details, visual imagery, and emotional impact. So imagine my delight when every person I interviewed for this book proved to be a master of this communication form. I knew I couldn't let their answers remain in my computer only. Thus, this chapter is devoted to those sage sound bites about what they have lived through and what they have learned over the course of their careers and in the midst of these tough times. Some of these quotes were used in the main body of the book. They bear repeating.

The quotations are arranged according to the following topics:
• Leadership
• Communication
• Motivation
• Stress
• Self-care
• Marketability and your career
• The boss's role
• The company's role
• Life

Live & Learn (cont.)

Leadership	People can handle the truth. They need to feel you're telling them the truth. Then trust develops.	Rex Heitz
	Leadership is about the future. Employees want to follow someone who is optimistic.	Ron Kirkpatrick
	Neutrality and empathy are two of the most critical leadership traits.	Maril MacDonald
	Who do you want to be? How do you want to see yourself? What kind of person do you want to be in this world, in this job, in this tough situation?	Maria Pozo-Humphreys
	Bad habits are created in good times. Good habits are created in bad times. This is a good quote to remember in this climate.	Ron Kirkpatrick
	People will work for a paycheck, but they will fight for a cause.	Maril MacDonald
	Managers who spend time learning about employees' hopes and fears can be much more effective.	Ron Kirkpatrick

Communication	Getting internal audiences on the right page is absolutely critical. We know the media is calling employees. If the employees know what is happening, any resulting news story will have better context.	Ron Culp
	In the absence of any response to a rumor, the rumor takes on more validity.	John Finney
	In tough times, people think about worst possible scenarios. The only way to counteract that is to have face-to-face meetings so employees can know the people making the decisions.	Ron Kirkpatrick
	Most problems are communication problems.	Natalie Wilson
	It's easy to have fire-up talks with my staff when there's good or exciting news. One of the things I have to realize is that I still have to communicate with the staff even when there isn't good news.	Natalie Wilson
	Bosses who are not comfortable delivering bad news try to dance around the topic and hope the person "gets it."	Karl Ahlrichs
	It is really important for owners or managers to get out in front of employees and talk about any issue that is bugging them. The more often you can do this, the fewer rumors there will be.	Ron Kirkpatrick

Communication (cont.)	No matter how good a communicator you are, you can't just swoop in from corporate headquarters and drop some news. No matter how brilliantly crafted or empathetic it is, you can't just walk away. The [repercussions] happen at the outside location.	Maril MacDonald
	Communication should not be episodic. It needs to be continual.	Mike Hanson
	There was a time when I didn't talk to employees much. I didn't want to get too close…but I've come full circle. Now I know employees want that relationship. They appreciate your knowledge, experience, and input.	Mark Eaton

Motivation	Most of us, whether we've articulated it or not, are on a mission. The successful companies are figuring out how to create a space where employees can feel like they're accomplishing their mission in the context of their job.	Maril MacDonald
	The key to communication is to make it as personal as it can be. Be honest. Bridge to a brighter future. Leave people with hope.	Ron Kirkpatrick
	Ownership of the solution is more important than the solution itself.	John McKinney
	High performers want to have a tough talk within 24 hours of the event you are evaluating. Then the annual performance review can be used for a future strategy session.	Karl Ahlrichs
	Motivation is a measurable list.	Mark Stadler
	Many companies look at employee retention and engagement around the aspect of compensation, benefits, and rewards, which are all extrinsic motivators. They ignore what intrinsically motivates people— those things that really get people up in the morning. Those are their dreams and hopes.	Maril MacDonald
	It's important to understand what motivates your boss.	Mike Hanson

Stress	When people live with a higher amount of stress than usual, they may stop exercising. They often grab food on the run and don't digest it well. They begin to live on coffee. This all contributes to their energy spiraling down and down.	Deborah Del Vecchio-Scully
	People frequently use distraction to avoid problems. Even if their minds are occupied by a TV show, the body still activates the stress response. The problem has not gone away. Distraction doesn't work for very long.	Deborah Del Vecchio-Scully
	When you take a couple of deep breaths, you can become more mindful and cultivate a response to the situation.	Deborah Del Vecchio-Scully
	The hardest part of a tough talk is tolerating what you feel about the message you are communicating.	Deborah Del Vecchio-Scully
	Internalizing, ignoring, or numbing your feelings doesn't work because they just go underground and come up at later, perhaps inappropriate, times.	Maria Pozo-Humphreys

Self-care	Part of the battle for me is to set aside time to let my mind catch up. Meditations help me process the day.	Ron Kirkpatrick
	It is important that the boss seek support from trusted friends before and after the tough talk to externalize his or her own feelings.	Maria Pozo-Humphreys
	Energy is your most valuable asset. Make sure you are managing your own energy so you can be at your best in difficult conversations.	Patti Ayars
	Great leaders have always needed retreats.	Ron Kirkpatrick
Marketability	Step outside your comfort zone. Take your boss to lunch. You know the company is struggling. Ask what you can do to help.	Mark Eaton
	What is the thing that you are more passionate about than anyone else?	Cali Williams Yost
	An interesting offset of the economic slowdown is that it gives you a chance to be creative. What worked before is not working now. Revisit your core passion and come up with a different strategy.	Mark Eaton

Your role as boss	Do you see yourself as a boss who can get business done and relate well to people and care about them? Or just as a boss who only sees bottom line?	Maria Pozo-Humphreys
	High performers respect a boss who develops them and calls them out when their work is just average.	Karl Ahlrichs
	When I have to discipline an employee, I first point out their strengths and compliment them on something they're doing well. Then I tell them where they need to step up to do a better job. I try to have them see the excitement in the job.	Natalie Wilson
	If someone were shocked by a decision we made, I would view it as a failure on my part, given the many opportunities we have to coach and the tools we have to succeed.	Mark Stadler
	You are dealing with the whole person. As a manager, you only get a glimpse of them. There is a whole lot under the surface. Things have gone on in the past that you, as manager, do not see. It's important for bosses to realize that it is not appropriate for them to practice psychotherapy.	Patti Ayars

We often focus on how hard it is for us to give a tough talk. It's important to realize we are serving a bigger purpose for a lot of people.	Patti Ayars
For the most part, your tough talk about a termination should not be a long conversation. Be honest and get to the point. Don't get into a debate.	Heidi Leithead
Early on in my career, I tried to have the initial meeting involving layoffs be detailed and lengthy and include all the information the employees would eventually want to know. But I learned that didn't work. I needed to make the initial meeting brief, then allow for follow-up later with the human resource professionals.	Rex Heitz
It's having a compassionate connection with the employee that helps him absorb the news. Also, showing faith in that person's ability to rebound is an important component.	Maria Pozo-Humphreys
Spend more time with your employees. Get to a deeper level than before. These times are stressful for everybody. It is in your best interests to pull together as a team. Everybody will win.	Mark Eaton

Your role as boss (cont.)	The receivers of the bad news need to understand they have responsibility for themselves. The boss can help reframe the bad news and should help them see that they are still connected and not isolated.	Maria Pozo-Humphreys
	Get out and hear what other small businesses are doing and engage your employees in conversation.	Mark Eaton
	Anyone who owns a dog knows that if you come home and the dog has knocked over the flowerpot earlier in the day, punishing it is useless. You have to do it immediately. The same is true of disciplinary actions or performance reviews. You have to do it fairly soon after problems occur. Otherwise, meaningful behavioral change will not happen.	Karl Ahlrichs
	Be clear about what you are trying to achieve — not just what to do but what to create.	Patti Ayars

The role of the company or organization	So often, legal considerations drive the process. Make sure the process pieces are balanced against the values of company.	Rose Gailey
	In large corporations there is often a small group of people who develop the strategy [for communicating bad news]. Those people have spent a lot of time understanding the issues, thinking through alternatives, etc. Ultimately, they come to a conclusion, then go out and explain the decision to others on a superficial level. Then they don't understand why the rest of the company isn't going from zero to 60 miles an hour.	Maril MacDonald
	A company should have agreements in place about confidentiality. Ideally, you have people sign them on their first day of employment so they understand their obligations to the company.	Heidi Leithead
	A lot of companies are cutting training departments [during these tough times]. I think that is the wrong place to cut. When you don't train the employees, the staff becomes stagnant. That is not the type of workforce that helps you become successful.	Chris Woolard

The role of the company or organization (cont.)	Regardless of the education level of their employees, it is the obligation of the people who run the company to do the best job they can of explaining of how the business works.	Ron Kirkpatrick
	Anything you say can, and will, go public. As you think about what you say, think about whether you can live with your words if they end up in the public domain.	Heidi Leithead
	Go back to the values of the company. The test of a truly healthy organizational culture is reflected in how you say goodbye to employees.	Rose Gailey
	Reducing staff is the reality of business [today]. Management has to engage people with the facts so they can understand what's happening, adapt, and protect themselves.	Mark Stadler
	Every company is struggling with the impact of social media. So everything must be transparent. This is hard for companies used to controlling information.	Ron Kirkpatrick
	Unions are very good at getting management to deliver the bad news and keeping the good news for themselves.	Maril MacDonald
	Companies often think the internal message and external message are the same. They're not. You must give more context to employees.	Ron Culp

Life	Treating people with respect is truly empowering. It equips us to handle difficult conversations with neutrality, a spirit of compassion, and clarity.	Rose Gailey
	In our lives we all remember the people who told us the truth in a diplomatic way.	Karl Ahlrichs
	It is hard to be grateful and judgmental at the same time, or to be grateful and angry at the same time. Gratitude allows you to be neutral and objective.	Rose Gailey
	A breakdown is sometimes the biggest opportunity for a breakthrough.	Patti Ayars
	Problems don't solve themselves; they just get bigger.	Natalie Wilson
	If you think you're in the wrong place, you probably are.	Mark Stadler
	Some nights the shots don't go in.	Mark Eaton
	How would you like to come to work and have no control? That is not healthy for people, families, or the community.	John McKinney

Life (cont.)	I take time to pray about [my tough talks]. I ask for clarity or peace of mind for people who hear the message and that I am able to convey to them the right message with dignity and respect. There are times I've changed my mind [on a business decision] as a result of praying and reflecting.	Mark Stadler
	We will all experience failures— things we are not very successful at. Do you let them set you back or do you utilize them to help you move forward? I say you should fail in a way that helps you move forward. Fail forward.	Patti Ayars
	People need to know you care about them and think they're important, even when you're delivering bad news. Sharing their disappointment and having faith in their ability to rebound is important.	Maria Pozo-Humphreys
	People want to know you care about them. If people feel cared for, they can deal with most anything.	Mark Eaton
	Sometimes, when there is a situation that is not working and you have put a lot of energy into it, ending the relationship is a relief for both parties.	Deborah Del Vecchio-Scully

Knowledge kills fear.	Ron Kirkpatrick
I worry that people who are not making sure these things [physical health, community ties, spiritual grounding] are a part of their lives will not survive tough times. It sounds really dramatic, but I don't want to underestimate how critical it is that we learn skills to take care of ourselves.	Cali Williams Yost
You can't manufacture performance or think for your people. They think on their own and come to their own conclusions.	John McKinney
Problems don't age well. So do what you need to do, process it, or debrief with a trusted colleague or friend and then move on.	Maria Pozo-Humphreys

There are many more notable quotations from the interviews. I will be posting them on the website, www.toughtalks.biz.

If you have a quote or sound bite you can add about tough talks you've had—as a recipient or as the deliverer, please e-mail me, send me a tweet, or post it on my blog. I look forward to hearing from you.

In the meantime, good luck on your next tough talk.

Jean Palmer Heck
Conference Speaker
International Communications Advisor

jean@toughtalks.biz
www.toughtalks.biz
www.twitter.com/toughtalks

Appendices

Works cited

Chapter 1

1. Quoted in Knowledge@Wharton's "How Small Companies Can Avoid HR Misunderstandings" on American Express OPEN Forum blog on December 29, 2008. Formerly available at: http://blogs.openforum.com/author/knowledgewharton

2. Adecco Group North America. "Hoping for Stabilization…Better Plan for Resignations." June 25, 2009. Available online at: http://www.adeccousa.com/articles/
Hoping-for-StabilizationBetter-Plan-for Resignations.html?id=112&url=/
pressroom/pressreleases/pages/forms/
allitems.aspx&templateurl=/
AboutUs/pressroom/Pages/Press-release.aspx

3. Author's interviews with Chris Woolard, Employee Loyalty Specialist, Walker Information. July 23, 2009. July 27, 2009.

Walker Information. "The Walker Loyalty Report for Loyalty in the Workplace." Indianapolis: 2007. Available online at: http://www.walkerinfo.com/pics/
wlr/Employee_ExecSumm_07.pdf

4. Watson Wyatt Worldwide. "Debunking the Myths of Employee Engagement." 2006/2007 WorkUSA® Survey Report. Available online at: http://www.watsonwyatt.com/research/
resrender.asp?id=2006-US-0039

Chapter 2

1. U.S. National Institute of Mental Health. "The Numbers Count: Mental Disorders in America." Washington, D.C.: 2008. Available online at: http://www.nimh.nih.gov/health/
publications/the-numbers-count-mental-disorders-in america/
index.shtml

2. Author's interviews with Rose Gailey, Maria Pozo-Humphreys, Deborah Del Vecchio-Scully, Patti Ayars. Numerous dates.

Works cited
(cont.)

Chapter 4

1. Maslow, Abraham H. "A Theory of Human Motivation." Psychological Review, 50, 370-396. 1943. Available online at http://psychclassics.yorku.ca/Maslow/motivation.htm

2. Watson Wyatt Worldwide. "2009/2010 Communication ROI Study: Advance Highlights." Available online at: http://www.watsonwyatt.com/CommROI/

3. Schaeffer, John. "Cash Just Isn't Enough." Schaefer Recognition Group, 2009. Available online at: http://www.schaeferrecognitiongroup.com/downloads/articles/Cash%20Just%20Isn%27t%20Enough.pdf

4. McLain is quoted in Jennifer Robison's "Building Engagement in this Economic Crisis." Gallup Management Journal, February 19, 2009. Available online at: http://gmj.gallup.com/content/115213/building-engagement-economic-crisis.aspx

5. Kawasaki, Guy. "The Art of Laying People Off." American Express OPEN Forum. November 18, 2008. Available online at: http://www.openforum.com/idea-hub/topics/the-world/article/the-art-of-laying-people-off

6. Deloitte & Touche USA LLP. "2007 Volunteer IMPACT Survey." Available online at: http://www.deloitte.com

Allen, Sharon. "Our new world: a turning point for corporate volunteerism." Speech at the National Conference on Volunteering and Service, San Francisco, CA, June 23, 2009.

7. Live United. CSR Research: Cause marketing--an effective investment. Available online at: http://www.liveunited.org/ncl/research.cfm

8. Kouzes, Jim. "Global Leadership Lesson #4: Exemplary Global Leaders are Inspiring." December 10, 2007. Available online at: http://www.amazon.com/gp/blog/post/PLNK1C2DFVA8F62UY

Chapter 5
1. Kawasaki, Guy. "The Art of Laying People Off." American Express OPEN Forum. November 18, 2008. Available online at: http://www.openforum.com/idea-hub/topics/theworld/article/the-art-of-laying-people-off

Appendices (cont.)

Resources

Biz Info Library is a searchable business resource archive. It covers topics from closing your business to human resources. Registration is required.
www.bizinfolibrary.org/

Emotional Intelligence Central, written by Dr. Jeanne Segal, a psychologist, offers a variety of free online courses about improving your emotional intelligence and dealing with workplace stress. The site also hosts reference material and videos.
www.emotionalintelligencecentral.org

The United States Office of Personnel Management, which manages the federal civilian workforce, offers a number of downloadable resources designed for federal workers that are adaptable to private organizations. The following website focuses on EAPs.
www.opm.gov/Employment_and_Benefits/WorkLife/HealthWellness/EAP/

Helpguide is a nonprofit organization whose mission is to provide up-to-date information about mental health and lifelong wellness. Its website offers numerous articles on psychological and medical issues with links to other applicable resources.
www.helpguide.org/mental/burnout_signs_symptoms.htm

WebMD® is a resource of health care information. The following web page addresses work-life balance issues.
www.webmd.com/balance/default.htm

Human Resource Executive Online™ is an interactive resource designed specifically for directors and vice presidents of HR. It is the online content provider for Human Resource Executive magazine. Content from Cornell University, webinars, and other resources are offered.
www.hreonline.com

Nolo.com is a website focusing on legal issues. Their offerings include articles, podcasts, forms, and books about the law. Some of the books may be available through your local library or through an inter-library loan.
www.nolo.com

The Service Corps of Retired Executives (SCORE) is a national association focused on helping small businesses form and grow. Free one-on-one business counseling services, as well as online counseling and workshops are provided in partnership with the U.S. Small Business Administration.
www.score.org

The U.S. Small Business Administration (SBA) exists solely to provide practical support for small businesses. Many local or regional SBA offices offer extensive libraries and training programs at either low or no cost.
www.sba.gov

Spirit & Work Business Center is Pat McHenry Sullivan's online resource for her work on re-visioning work. She offers practical tools for finding your vocation, bringing faith and integrity into the workplace, creating balance, and achieving work-life excellence.
www.workwithmeaningandjoy.com

Workforce Management Magazine offers free access to thousands of articles, tips, policies, forms, and e-mail newsletters covering a variety of business topics, including benefits and staffing.
www.workforce.com

Recommended reading

Ambrose, Delorese. *Healing the Downsized Organization: What Every Employee Needs to Know About Today's New Workplace.* New York: Three Rivers Press, 1996.

Ayars, Patti J. *The Art of Leading Transformational Change.* Bloomington, Indiana: AuthorHouse, 2009.
http://www.turningpoint-consulting.com/resources/

Clarke-Epstein, Chris. *78 Important Questions Every Leader Should Ask and Answer.* New York: AMACOM, 2006.
http://www.change101.com

Recommended reading (cont.)

Glanz, Barbara A. *Handle With CARE: Motivating and Retaining Employees.* New York: McGraw-Hill, 2002. http://www.barbaraglanz.com/

Hathaway, Patti. *Secrets to Unleashing Employee Greatness: The Step-by-Step System to Maximize Every Employee's Performance.* Van Nuys, California: Destination Publications, 2005. http://www.techsn.com/thechangeagent/

Kouzes, James M. and Barry Z. Posner. *Credibility: How Leaders Gain and Lose It, Why People Demand It.* San Francisco: Jossey-Bass Publisher, 1993.

———. *The Leadership Challenge: How to Keep Getting Extraordinary Things Done in Organizations.* San Francisco: Jossey-Bass Publisher, 1995.

Noer, David M. *Healing the Wounds: Overcoming the Trauma of Layoffs and Revitalizing Downsized Organizations.* San Francisco: Jossey-Bass Publisher, 1993.

Tieger, Paul D. and Barbara Barron. *Do What You Are: Discover the Perfect Career for You Through the Secrets of Personality Type.* 4th ed. New York: Little, Brown and Company, 2007.

Stone, Douglas, Bruce Patton and Sheila Heen. *Difficult Conversations: How to Discuss What Matters Most.* New York: Penguin, 2000.

Vinitsky, Michael H. and Ayars, Patti J. *Mastering Momentum: A Practical and Powerful Approach for Successful Change.* San Diego, California: Momentum Organization Consultants, 2000. http://www.turningpoint-consulting.com/resources/

Walton, Mark S. *Generating Buy-In: Mastering the Language of Leadership.* New York: AMACOM, 2004.

Yost, Cali Williams. *Work+Life: Finding the Fit That's Right for You.* New York: Riverhead Books, 2004. http://www.worklifefit.com/

Take a two-minute retreat	©*Pat McHenry Sullivan, 1995, originally published for the Brobeck, Phleger & Harrison newsletter*

You need a break. Your co-workers wish you would take that break. But you don't have the money or time for a proper break.

Fortunately, using nothing but your imagination, you can obtain some benefits of an extended break without leaving your desk.

There's probably no better stress buster than imagination. It's free, fun. and easy to use, and it's something you always have with you. It can help lower blood pressure, enhance your immune system, reverse heart disease and cancer, and relax computer-fogged eyes.

As Allied European commander in World War II and as President of the United States, Dwight D. Eisenhower encountered at least as much stress as the average worker today. Ike reportedly liked to imagine himself on his favorite hole of his favorite golf course. That simple imaginary retreat gave him the perspective and focus he needed to think more clearly during stressful times.

In your imaginary retreat, reality is not an issue. The only thing that matters is that you design a setting that's perfect for you. If you wish, you can have a room with a view high in the Alps next to an ocean beach. You can have a relaxing massage from Denzel Washington followed by a vigorous workout led by Tina Turner. You can have total quiet or a private concert by Ludwig von Beethoven.

In your retreat, you don't have to be nice or positive. That's why you can have a Virtual Reality Room where you can slowly roast a troublesome adversary over a blue flame, without the slightest actual consequences to you or said adversary.

Imagine staying in your retreat long enough for the tension to drain out of your bones. Imagine watching your zombie-like stare turn to alertness. Imagine hearing your voice change from crabby

Take a two-minute retreat (cont.)

to cheerful, your muscles becoming alive and strong again. Imagine compassion for yourself and others flowing through your body, mind and spirit.

Imagine that, in your relaxed state, you see your job from a fresh perspective. Imagine how you can tackle your work with more efficiency and resourcefulness. Imagine seeing your former adversaries through the eyes of compassion and creativity. Let yourself see how to bless and release them in a way that also respects you and lets you go about your business with integrity.

Come back to the present reality and go to work. You'll probably be more relaxed and focused, therefore more efficient.

Don't use this fantasy for the first time in the midst of a tight deadline! Also, don't use it while driving or otherwise engaged in something that needs your full attention. Instead, practice first during relaxed down time.

With practice, it's possible to feel as if you've had an extended retreat yet actually be away from work for no more than two minutes. It's also possible that, while imagining your perfect retreat, you'll discover simple ways to create more retreat time in your real life.

Pat McHenry Sullivan is an expert in spirit and work and author of many books and articles on the subject. To contact her, call 510-530-0284, or see www.workwithmeaningandjoy.com.

Index

Acknowledgments

The wonderful people who have come into my life as *Tough Talks in Tough Times* developed this year have been a blessing of overwhelming proportions. I am extremely thankful, and humbled by, all the encouragement, insights, connections, and stories from friends and strangers (on trains and planes) alike. No matter where I went, doors kept opening, allowing me in.

There are many people I would like to thank. Let me do so somewhat chronologically.

This book started with a conversation over dinner at a National Speakers Association conference. Mark LeBlanc, a small business growth expert, knew of the need for this topic and, familiar with my background in communications, thought I should write it. Saying it was a natural topic for my speaking business, he spent a few hours with me and helped me with the plans needed to take on this big project. I am so grateful for his ideas. This book has become much more than a project. It is now a mission to help people through the difficult conversations at work and in life.

During the initial interviews I explored the topic with three people whom I know personally and greatly admire, Maria Pozo-Humphreys, Natalie Wilson, and Karl Ahlrichs. Their expertise on the subject matter helped me to put this big idea into a logical framework.

During the initial conversations, I also talked with my former boss, longtime friend, and corporate communuication/public relations guru, Ron Culp. He had great ideas, was excited about the topic, and put me in touch with many of the people interviewed for this book. Not only that, his encouragement was unending over the months it took to research and write the book. Just when I thought this book was taking me much too long to get in print, he would send an e-mail saying he was amazed at my progress. Exactly what I needed at those points. In addition, he was willing to brainstorm any time I needed his expertise.

Acknowledgments (cont.)

Kathy Loveless was also at the beginning of this project encouraging me. She graciously opened her home to me for a personal writing retreat. The view of the Wasatch Mountains from her house always inspires me, as does the inner and outer beauty of Kathy. She is a dear friend and the genius behind my mastermind group of Jim Ackerman, Mark Eaton, Marc Wohlsfeld, and Jeff Fleming, who also gave me good advice.

My weekly meetings back in Indiana with Elaine Morrison, Jody Springer, and Natalie Wilson gave me such a lift. They have shared their businesses and lives with me. I am lucky to have their love and friendship. They have become my soul sisters.

My sincere thanks goes to all the people interviewed for the book, including those previously mentioned and Patti Ayars, Bob Borden, Mike Cutler, Deborah Del Vecchio-Scully, Mark Eaton, Carol Fredrickson, Rose Gailey, Janet Giesselman, Briana Hanson, Pam Gilley, Nido Quebin, Mike Hanson, Steven Hanson, Rex Heitz, Megan Johnson, Ron Kirkpatrick, Bill Kuhl, Regina Laux, Heidi Leithead, Seralynn Lewis, Maril MacDonald, John McKinney, Bob Postlethwait, Mark Stadler, Charlotte Weeks, Chris Woolard, Bill Yeargin, and Cali Yost.

They spent many hours sharing their expertise and never complained when I would follow up to ensure all the quotes were exactly as spoken or interpreted.

I appreciate Pat McHenry Sullivan's allowing me to reprint "The Two-Minute Vacation" for you. She has also served as an excellent researcher.

The book looks the way it does because of the talents of Meta4 Design, a well-respected firm located in Chicago. When I first met Joan Link and Fred Biliter and saw their previous work, I knew they could take my words and showcase them so you, the reader, would get the most from them. Since "communicate visually" is one of my mantras, I wanted this book to be as easy to use — and peruse — as possible. Meta4 has certainly done that — and more. The CHECK process, and all that goes into it, is made so much clearer because of their stellar work. Every communicator should have partners like Meta4 at their side. In addition, Meta4's Jerry Lenz and Andrew Biliter have been a part of the production and I thank them for their tireless behind-the-scenes efforts.

Linda Jackson, APR, a professional and personal friend, has added her public relations acumen to the success of this book. Many more people will read it because of all she is doing to get the word out. Her intelligence, work ethic, and gentle nature are such a gift.

Carrie Lambert, my assistant, is the one who keeps me on track. Her organizational skills and energy make her a joy to work with.

The yeoman's work on editing has fallen on my son, Tim. When the book was in the final editing stages, so skillfully started by Barbara McNichol, Captain Heck had just returned from Afghanistan and finished his four-year commitment to the United States Marine Corps. I knew he was an excellent writer and editor and was thrilled that he agreed to take a look at it. He did more than look. The book you are reading is much more refined because of his work. I'm trying to tempt him to edit future *Tough Talks* books, but I believe there is a different call awaiting him. Great news for his next employer. Not so good news for me.

I appreciate all the help my extended family has given me, as they have listened, commented, proofread, reviewed, shared, and encouraged. A loving thanks to Jim, Barb, Bobbie, Barbara, Andy, Amy, Francois, and Zach.

The exuberance and unconditional love from my daughter, Laura, and mother, Ann Palmer, have always been a spark for me. Their unstoppable energy and contagious personailties bring such joy. Their spirit has been with me throughout. It's a special blessing that they live less than five miles away and drop in with smiles on their faces regularly.

Acknowledgements (cont.)

Finally, Gary, the love of my life for 28 years, has supported me in ways I can't even count. This latest undertaking of mine would have taxed most spouses. But not Gary. He cooked dinner, did the laundry, kept the household running, and gave me as much "writer's space" as I needed. All the time doing massive amounts of volunteer work for the community. And he has asked for nothing in return…except the promise that I'll take back the cooking chores! (Next week, dear.)

From the bottom of my heart to all who have been a part of this book, I thank you.

Jean Palmer Heck

About the author

What if...
- You had to deliver bad news to employees, motivate them so the company wouldn't fold, and keep your own stress level in check?
- Your company stood to lose one of its biggest sources of income because a customer had already decided your product wasn't needed?
- You read a news story about your company that was negative and filled with juicy quotes from an opposing attorney?

These are all communication issues — all real situations — and all ending with positive outcomes because of Jean Palmer Heck, an international communications advisor.

Heck has taken her skills as a strategist, TV news anchor and corporate spokesperson — and her connections with top-level executives — to analyze the good, the bad, and the ugly about delivering tough talks in tough times and developed the CHECK system to help people through them. She designed a presentation that has had a multimillion-dollar impact on a major corporation. And she has fine-tuned her 3-D Sound Bite System to neutralize negative media coverage.

Heck has spent 30 years working with worldwide newsmakers and senior executives from 32 countries. An executive coach and consultant for numerous corporations, including Eli Lilly, Verizon, Praxair, GTE, and Arthur Andersen, Heck has spoken to hundreds of audiences and trains all levels of management. Heck has been a radio/TV news anchor and talk show host as well as a corporate spokesperson on controversial issues. She is an avid videographer and travels around the world to gather award-winning footage for her speeches.

In addition to *Tough Talks in Tough Times: What Bosses Need to Know to Deliver Bad News, Motivate Employees & Stay Sane*, Heck is author of

- *Secrets for the Reluctant Speaker*
- *Sound Bites for Top Dogs*
- *Chicken Soup for the Soul* (contributor to two books)
- *The Presentation Tool Box*
- *Powerful Presentation Road Maps*
- *Bloom How You're Planted*

For more information, contact Jean Palmer Heck at jean@toughtalks.biz.

Seminars and Training

Jean Palmer Heck speaks at local, national, and international conferences. She provides breakout sessions, training workshops, and keynote addresses, accompanied by learning resources. All of her programs are customized for each audience.

If you are interested in booking Jean Palmer Heck to speak, please contact her at speaking@toughtalks.biz.